The Myth of Racial Supremacy

Restoring the African Mind Research Collection

1 ON WESTERN CIVILIZATION AND THE BIRTH OF WHITE SUPREMACY

Western civilization is a rather interesting topic to address because views on this topic are shaped by the perspective one uses to judge what is known as civilization. Obviously, Western civilization has given birth to many great technological advancements, many great philosophical concepts, and many great examples of art. At the same time, it is also true that Western civilization has been responsible for many great atrocities as well. The statement here is not unique to Western civilization. Western civilization is not the only civilization which has committed atrocities, but I mentioned the atrocities to make the point that the topic of Western civilization can be a complex one because of these two conflicting realities of what Western civilization has been.

I am an African who was born in a former European colony. I state this at the onset to make the point that my very existence is rooted in the historical legacy of Western colonialism. I was born in Guyana and Guyana itself is a product of this legacy of colonialism. Western civilization has left an undeniable global impact on peoples across the world, yet this has not always been a positive impact. My African ancestors were stolen from their African homelands and enslaved in the Americas. I also have Amerindian ancestry. Amerindians were dispossessed of their lands as European colonizers took control. I have Indian ancestry as well. Indians were not only colonized, but my Indian ancestors were brought to Guyana as indentured laborers where they endured brutalities as well. Flowing through my blood is a lengthy history of abuse which was carried out by Europeans.

I am not suggesting that Europeans were the only ones to have ever done bad things in history. Africans waged wars on each other which often resulted in death and destruction. Most of the Africans who were captured and enslaved in the Americas were sold by other Africans. Amerindians also waged wars on each other, as did Indians. War, conquest, and slavery are human traits which are not unique to European societies. I want to state this early on, so critics of my position cannot accuse me of trying to propagate the view that the various ills of Western civilization are unique only to

Western civilization.

I am also not denying the great things which Western civilization has produced, yet I also have to deal with the reality that as an African from a former colony, Western civilization has never been my civilization. I come from a people who have been victims of Western civilization. I come from a people who have suffered the worst aspects of Western civilization. This was the point that Malcolm X made about being an African in America. He stated that African Americans have not enjoyed the fruits of Americanism. Rather, they have only known the thorns. This has been the general situation of African people where Western civilization is concerned. The lofty ideals about democracy, liberty, and the rights of man have never been extended to us.

Among some Westerners there has been an attempt to distance Western civilization itself from the crimes of colonialism. M. Mannoni, for example, wrote that European civilization and its best representatives are not responsible for colonial racialism. To this, Frantz Fanon quoted Francis Jeanson who noted that certain French citizens prided themselves in keeping a distance from colonialism. Jeanson noted that it was the "blind indifference" of French citizens which allowed thugs to carry out the deeds which they did. Colonialism is Western civilization. There is no way to separate the two. Colonialism was carried out not only by the leaders of Western civilization, but also through citizens who prided themselves in keeping their distance from the crimes committed by their government.

Before I get deep into the discussion about Western civilization, I think it is first necessary to state what I mean by Western civilization. Western civilization refers to a collection of the nations which emerged in Europe. As European settlers moved to the Americas, they also brought their culture and worldview with them, which expanded Western civilization beyond the geographic location of Europe. The concept of Western civilization is essentially one which seeks to create a unifying identity for the diverse ethnic groups and nationalities which originate in Europe. The concept is also one which sets the West apart from the rest of the world. The history of Western civilization is one which is filled with conflicts and clashes between various Western states, so it is not as though the West has always been united, but the concept of a collective Western civilization is how the West has set itself apart from the rest of the world. This became especially necessary during the age of colonialism when Western states sought to conquer the rest of the world.

The concept of Western civilization is also related to the concept of race. Humans have always recognized differences in physical traits and cultural traits, but race is a concept which emerged within Western civilization during the age of colonialism to justify the Western colonization of people who were not deemed to be white. White itself represented the physical appearances of Europeans who recognized that the complexions of others around the world were much darker than their own. Out of this concept of race came racism, which was built on the notion white people were a superior race and that people should be defined by their racial identity. Out of racism emerged systems such as Jim Crow and apartheid, which upheld white supremacy at the expense of black people who were deemed to be inferior.

It is important to note here that racism may have been one of Western civilization's negative aspects, but racism in Western civilization was not a feature which was present in its early Greco-Roman roots. Frank Snowden demonstrated that in ancient Greco-Roman society, there was no prejudice associated with skin color. Snowden explained that "both Greeks and Romans, notwithstanding a few concepts and ideas sometimes misinterpreted as anti-black in sentiment, had the ability to see and to comment on the obviously different physical characteristics of Ethiopians without developing an elaborate and rigid system of discrimination based on the color of the skin." Color prejudice in Europe did become more noticeable. In one of his lectures, Eusi Kwayana noted that in William Shakespeare's play, *The Merchant of Venice*, a man from Morocco seeks to marry a woman named Portia. Much of their interaction was centers on the complexion of the Moroccan man, who asks Portia to mislike him not because of his dark complexion. The Moroccan man fails in his attempt to marry Portia because he selects the wrong casket. This causes Portia to remark, "Let all of his complexion choose me so." Kwayana mentioned this to show that prejudice based on skin color did exist in Europe before racism became institutionalized.

James Sweet argued that racial prejudice was introduced to Europe by the Moors when the Moors had conquered Iberia. As Sweet noted, Arabs developed their own racist views against African people. Sweet argued that "many Iberian Christians had internalized the racist attitudes of the Muslims and were applying them to the increasing flow of African slaves to their part of the world." This seems plausible, but my focus here is not so much on where racism in Western civilization emerged from. My point is that racism was not a feature of Western civilization in the early development of Western civilization. Racism became more prominent in the 1500s and onward.

The notion of racial superiority has been connected to the concept of Western superiority. Sam Francis expressed this view when he stated: "The civilization that we as whites created in Europe and America could not have developed apart from the genetic endowments of the creating people, nor is there any reason to believe that the civilization can be successfully transmitted by a different people." According to Patrick Buchanan, Francis was "suggesting Western civilization was superior and that only Europeans could have created it."

The question is why would such a suggestion need to be made? There is no question that white people created Western civilization, but it has never been enough for Westerners to feel content with the civilization which they created for themselves. There has always been a sense of superiority over other civilizations which has driven a desire to conquer other civilizations and to impose Western cultural norms on those conquered people.

This sense of superiority was also reinforced through denying the historical achievements of others. An example of this was the civilization of Great Zimbabwe in Africa. Its historical achievements were attributed to Phoenicians to avoid giving credit to African people. This view was challenged by Peter Garlake. This brought Garlake into conflict with Ian Smith's government. Smith hired individuals to challenge Garlake's conclusions. Garlake was forced into exile in 1970 simply for daring to write the truth about the history of Great Zimbabwe. In an obituary for

Garlake titled "Peter Garlake (1934-2011), Great Zimbabwe and the politics of the past in Zimbabwe," Innocent Pikirayi wrote that "Peter Garlake enjoyed considerable international recognition for the high quality and impact of his recent research, all of which indicated his standing as a leading international scholar." This was also precisely why the government of Rhodesia opposed his work.

One point which caught my attention upon revisiting Buchanan's work was his claim that the genocide in Rwanda and Burundi represented the "long and bloody history" of the Tutsi and Hutu people. Buchanan was mistaken. The history of the Tutsi and Hutu was not long and bloody at all. In fact, prior to European colonization, the dividing line was between Rwanda and Burundi, not Tutsi and Hutu. The tribal conflict was one which was instigated by the colonial powers. I make this point here to show that in the process of spreading its civilization to other people, the colonial powers created a great deal of instability and conflict. This is not to suggest that Africans were living in utopian societies before Europeans arrived, but colonialism certainly did no favors for Africa.

One of the worst examples of this was in the nation which would become known as Namibia. The Germans committed genocide. For several years, Germany did not even acknowledge the genocide nor did Germany offer an apology. Germany has also refused to pay reparations for the genocide. The genocide in Namibia was followed by the genocide of the Jews in Germany many years later. This is the product of a civilization which creates a distinction between superior people and inferior people who are worthy of being eliminated.

African people have often pondered on the roots of this racist and violent behavior. Elijah Muhammad claimed that white people were created to be a race of devils by a scientist named Yakub. Dr. Bobby E. Wright offered a more scientific explanation by suggesting that European behavior reflected an "underlying biologically transmitted proclivity" which was rooted "deep in their evolutionary history." Dr. Frances Cress Welsing argued that racism was motivated by a fear of white genetic annihilation. She argued that white people are not only a global minority, but that they are also genetically recessive. This view would certainly explain the white supremacist opposition to miscegenation—

although some white supremacists advocated for miscegenation to eliminate the African population. Welsing also argued that white racism specifically targeted black males because black males posed a threat to white genetic survival.

In *How Europe Underdeveloped Africa*, Walter Rodney, utilizing a Marxist analysis of history, traced the roots of racism in Europe to slavery and the emergence of capitalism. He noted that the enslavement of African people was not done for racist reasons, but rather that racism developed as a means to rationalize the enslavement of African people. As the capitalist system developed, Rodney noted that racism became an integral part of the capitalist mode of production. Rodney was also careful to point out that it would be too sweeping a statement to suggest that all racial prejudice in Europe derived from the enslavement of Africans and the exploitation of other non-white groups. The example he gave was anti-Semitism in Europe, which predated capitalism. This would suggest that racial prejudice in Europe became part of the mode of production due to colonialism and the emergence of capitalism, but that within Western society there was already a tendency towards extreme prejudice towards other groups.

The idea of race itself is not so much the problem. Physical differences exist. The problem with white supremacy is that white supremacists believe that differences suggest that there must be inferior and superior races. On his hajj to Mecca, Malcolm X shared the profound experience of worshiping alongside white people. Malcolm had believed Elijah Muhammad's teachings that white people were devils by nature, but his experience in Mecca brought him in contact with people who were physically white, but to them being white represented incidental characteristics. Malcolm contrasted this with white identity in American society, in which white means "boss." White within a white supremacist society is not merely an incidental physical trait, but a social status which represents power and domination.

As I will demonstrate here, race as a concept is one which is not only biological, but cultural as well. It is for this reason that roots of Western civilization and the roots of white identity can be traced to a process of historical development in Europe by which

Europeans or white people came to develop a sense of a collective identity. This sense of a shard white identity was one which distinguished white people and Western civilization from the other peoples and civilizations of the world. To be white and to be a Westerner then not only defines Europeans as a group in relation to each other, but it also defines Europeans as a group in relation to the rest of the world which fell outside of the category of white.

Greco-Roman civilization forms the basis of what is known as Western civilization. It is for this reason that to understand Western civilization, one must understand ancient Greece and Rome. I stated earlier that what is known as Western civilization generally refers to the nations of Europe, but Greece and Rome were part of the Mediterranean world which expanded beyond Europe to include North Africa and West Asia. This interaction with these societies did shape Greece and Rome in important ways. This is also significant because the proponents of this notion that Western civilization represents a superior civilization would have to acknowledge that the roots of Western civilization did not emerge in isolation from other civilizations in the world, particularly those in North Africa and Western Asia.

George M. James argued in *Stolen Legacy* that Greek philosophy was stolen from the Egyptians. His aim in this book was to challenge the view that black people are "backward in culture and have made no contribution to civilization". I maintain that James may have been overstating the case to claim that Greeks stole their philosophy from the Egyptians, but I do think the point does stand that Egyptian civilization predated Greek civilization and that Greek society was hostile to philosophers. I do not think the Greek hostility towards philosophers necessarily indicates that the philosophers were preaching alien ideas which they took from Africa, but it does indicate the level of hostility which Western societies have often displayed towards new ideas which challenge the existing status quo. James noted: "Only a brief study of history is necessary to show that Greek philosophers were undesirable citizens, who throughout the period of their investigations were victims of relentless persecution, at the hands of the Athenian government. Anaxagoras was imprisoned and exiled; Socrates was executed; Plato was sold into slavery and Aristotle was indicted and exiled; while the earliest of them all, Pythagoras, was expelled from Croton in Italy."

Socrates was sentenced for committing the crime of not believing in the gods of the city and for introducing new divinities. He was also accused of corrupting the youth. Socrates' crime was that he dared to introduce new ideas which challenged the existing ideas. Socrates was made to kill himself by drinking poison, which he apparently did cheerfully.

It was not Socrates alone who was persecuted for his teachings. As James pointed out, Plato was sold into slavery and Aristotle was exiled. This is indicative of the fact that Western civilization has historically been hostile to new ideas. In prior writings, I have mentioned Giordano Bruno being killed by the Catholic Church for his scientific views. Bruno was arrested and charged with blasphemy. After a seven year trial, Bruno refused to recant his views. He was sentenced to death on January 20, 1600. Bruno was gagged so that he could not speak. He was then burned alive at the stake.

Ancient Greece was a collection of independent city-states. In *The Mediterranean World in Ancient Times*, Eva Matthews Sanford explained that the city-states "contrasted with the oriental monarchies, in which the city was subordinate to the royal power, and with the less civilized peoples who did not develop politically beyond a tribal organization." Sanford also noted that not all Western states developed in the same manner that the Greek city-states did. Epirus, for example, maintained a government of tribal kings. In this essay I draw a lot from Sanford's book because it provides a chronology of the history of civilizations in the Mediterranean world of which Greece and Rome were part of. Sanford also does a great job at detailing the social and political organization of Greece and Rome.

Within the city-states, aristocracies emerged. The aristocracy was to represent "the rule of the best," although the aristocracy began to break down as wealth began to overshadow birth. In some cases, men of ordinary birth were able to accumulate wealth through industry and commerce. Thus, aristocracy gave way to oligarchy, in which political rights were based on wealth rather than birth. What followed was political unrest which resulted in individuals seizing control of their cities and ruling as what became known as tyrants.

Aristotle defined tyranny as monarchy which ruled in the interest of the monarch alone without any regard for the community. Sanford noted that tyrants still depended on popular support against the opposition of the former rulers. The tyrant needed to ensure that he had soldiers to carry out a military coup if necessary. Tyrants were also known to increase their wealth by seizing the estates of aristocrats. Sanford noted the specific case of Orthagoras, who led a farmer's revolt against the aristocracy and established the longest uninterrupted tyranny in Greek history.

Athens stands out among the Greek city-states for its democratic government. Solon was a statesman in Athens who was appointed to resolve the economic and political crisis in Athens. Solon engaged in constitutional reforms which assisted the poor. This included cancelling all debts. Not only were all those who had been enslaved for debt freed, but enslavement for debt was prohibited. It was noted that Solon did not establish Athenian democracy, but his reforms prepared the way for it by giving people more power. Solon also held the view that the "people will follow its leaders best if it is neither given excessive liberty nor subjected to undue oppression."

It was the reforms of Cleisthenes which led to the emergence of democracy in Athens. Cleisthenes was a tyrant who played a leading role in Hellenic politics. He became the most powerful man in Athens following a period of strife. He also reformed the political structure of Athens by breaking up old factions. A council of 500 known as the boule was put in place as well. Fifty of its members were chosen by a lot from each of the ten tribes to serve for an annual term. Any Athenian citizen might be called to preside over the general assembly of the senate.

In addition to Athens, Sparta was another powerful Greek city-state. Sparta became a wealthy state following the conquest of Messenia. The land of Messenia was allotted to the helots who tilled it for the Spartans. The Spartan system of government was one in which two kings were chosen from the two royal families. Women in Sparta enjoyed more freedom than women in most other Greek cities, although they rarely saw their husbands—the condition of women in most Greek societies was reflected in

Aristotle's *Generation of Animals*, in which he stated females are deformed males. Sparta was a warrior society in which from the age of seven, boys were raised in military bands. Cowardice was abhorred in Spartan society. A man who displayed cowardice in battle was stripped of citizenship. Spartan mothers were free to kill their sons for being cowardly.

The Greek conflict with the Persian empire was an important conflict in Greece's history. The Greek city-states were disunited, but the threat posed by the Persian Empire forced the city-states to unite against a common enemy. The Persian dynasty was founded by Achaemenes. In time, the Persian state expanded through conquest and during the short reign of Cambyses, Persia annexed Egypt.

The conflict between Greece and Persia was sparked when the Ionian Greeks rebelled against Persia in 499 B.C. Aristagoras led this revolt. This revolt was put down by the Persians, despite the support that it received from Athens and Eretria. After suppressing the rebellion, Darius decided to send a punitive expedition to Greece. Greek and Persian forces clashed in 490 B.C. at the Battle of Marathon. This battle was a victory for the Athenians who were able to repel the Persians.

After Marathon, Darius' attention turned to Egypt where a revolt had broken out. Darius died in 486 B.C. and was succeeded by Xerxes who was occupied with subduing Egypt and Babylonia. Greece was given a ten year respite before having to confront the Persian Empire again in 480 B.C. The Greeks ultimately defeated the Persians.

One of the most significant moments in the conflict between the Persians and the Greeks was the battle at Thermopylae. This battle is notable for the stand made by Leonidas and his 300 Spartan warriors. These warriors, along with about 6,000 other Greek soldiers, stood up against a larger Persian army under the leadership of Xerxes. The Persians won the battle, but the Greek forces inflicted heavy casualties on the Persian forces. Herodotus reported that Xerxes lost so many men in the battle that he hid his dead so that no one could see how many Persians were killed by so few men. The stand which Leonidas and his Spartan warriors made not only came to represent what a Spartan warrior should be, but Leonidas became a symbol of Western freedom. This is why Sir William Golding wrote: "A little of Leonidas lies in the fact that I can go where I like and write what I like. He contributed to setting us free."

The Greek victory over the Persians was made possible by the unity of the Greek city-states, including Athens and Sparta. The unity produced by this war was not to last, however. This is demonstrated by the Peloponnesian War which was fought between Athens and the Peloponnesian League which included Sparta. The sessions of the Peloponnesian League were hosted in Sparta and Sparta also commanded the army of the league. The first Peloponnesian War began in 460 B.C. This conflict ended with the signing of a peace treaty in 445 B.C. War broke out again between the Peloponnesians and Athens. The Peloponnesian League ultimately prevailed over Athens in the second war.

Isocrates, who was a Greek orator, stands out for his advocacy of Greek unity. He believed that the role of Athens was the proper leader of this envisioned union. He saw interstate rivalry among Greek city-states as being ruinous. In his view, unity was needed for "the most necessary and righteous war which we wage in alliance with the Hellenes against the barbarians, who are by nature our foes and are eternally plotting against us." Isocrates eventually turned to Philip to undertake the effort of uniting the Greeks. Phillip was a Macedonian leader who was able to unite Greece under his authority. Phillip was eventually assassinated and he was succeeded by his son Alexander.

Alexander, who became known as Alexander the Great, emerged as one of history's great conquerors. He ascended to the throne of Macedonia following the assassination of his father and proceeded to build a large impure. Alexander's conquests included taking control of Egypt, which had been under Persian rule. Alexander accepted the crown of Upper and Lower Egypt, and was enthroned as pharaoh under the protection of Horus. Alexander was viewed as the son of Amun, whom the Greeks identified with Zeus. Alexander was addressed as the son of Zeus Amun. That Alexander embraced the religion of Egypt is interesting given the fact that the European colonial powers which colonized Africa many centuries later would impose their own cultural traditions on

Africans rather than embracing African cultural traditions in the manner which Alexander did.

Alexander died in 323 B.C. The empire which he built fragmented. The significance of Alexander the Great in European history is that he was the first great conqueror to emerge out of Europe who built a massive empire. Western civilization has given rise to a number of massive empires. This tradition began with Alexander the Great who expanded his empire into Asia and Africa. The empire which Alexander built would later be surpassed by the size of Rome.

As was noted, the Greeks and Romans did not perceive themselves as being white nor did they display the type of racist attitudes which would later emerge in the West. What the racist colonial empires of the West did draw from Greece and Rome—apart from the intellectual, cultural, and political traditions of Greece and Rome—was the drive for aggressive imperial expansion. This is what Alexander the Great was engaged in and it was what the Roman Empire was engaged in.

Rome was initially ruled by kings until the republic was established in 509 B.C. The republic was established by a bloodless revolution which expelled Tarquin the Proud. The senate in Rome served as the chief governing body of the republic. Two consuls were elected annually from the patrician families. Each consul held absolute authority, which included being able to have any citizen summarily executed or scourged. Each consul was also given the authority to veto the action of the other. In times of a political or military crisis, a dictator was appointed and given absolute authority over the two consuls. The dictator gave up power when the crisis was over.

The term dictator now carries a negative connotation because dictators tend to be leaders who have absolute power, which they abuse at the expense of their citizens. The Roman concept of dictatorship was that in times of extreme crisis, the dictator would temporarily seize power to resolve the situation. The dictator was not meant to have absolute power for life, but this is what dictatorship eventually came to be for many societies which have had dictators. As will be demonstrated, even in Rome itself the notion of having temporary dictators allowed room for the development of an empire which supplanted the republic.

The republic in Rome eventually came to an end due to the internal struggles over power in Rome. Julius Caesar joined with Crassus and Pompey to form what became known as the First Triumvirate. Together, the three men dominated Rome. The trio formed a temporary union to achieve their goals. Together, they secured a consulship for Caesar in 59 B.C. along with Bibulus. Caesar's status also increased following his conquest of Gaul, which further expanded Roman territory.

The Triumvirate eventually broke up. As Caesar was involved in his campaign in Gaul, Pompey was made the sole consul by the senate in order to restore order in Rome following the fights between Clodius' followers and rivals hired by Milo. By this time, Crassus had been killed in combat. As Pompey's political influence in Rome increased, Caesar found himself in political trouble after he was declared a public enemy. When this news reached Caesar, he decided to cross the river Rubicon. Marching an army into Roman territory was an act of war. The civil war which followed resulted in Caesar seizing power in Rome. He was granted dictatorship for ten years in 46 B.C. and then for life in 44 B.C. Caesar also had the right to express his opinion first in senatorial debates, to make war and peace without consulting the senate, and he was given complete control over the treasury.

Caesar's rule came to a violent end. The assassination of Caesar not only impacted Rome, it had implications for Egypt as well given that Caesar had a relationship with Cleopatra VII, which produced a child. Following Caesar's death, Cleopatra returned from Rome to Egypt and met Mark Antony in Syria. Cleopatra aligned herself with Mark Antony.

Following Caesar's assassination, his grandnephew Octavian rose to power in Rome and eventually became the first emperor in the history of the Roman Empire. He eventually clashed with Mark Antony over power in Rome. Octavian's forces defeated Antony's forces. Antony committed suicide and Cleopatra did the same. Following this, Egypt was annexed by Rome and came under Octavian's control.

Octavian was given the name Augustus by the senate. He was also called the principate. Augustus was granted greater powers.

Augustus claimed that he had restored the republic by transferring his power to the senate, although the power of the senate had been reduced. Augustus carried out a purge of the senate and reduced its size. Augustus also controlled foreign policy and treaties.

The Roman republic developed as a response to one-man rule which had been overthrown. The problem was that the republic still left space for one individual to seize power and rule as a dictator. As I stated previously, this was intended to be a temporary position, but Caesar exploited this position to make himself dictator for life. Caesar's dictatorship signaled the decline of the republic and the transition towards empire.

Nero, who began his rule in 54, was one of the most infamous emperors in the history of the Roman Empire. One of the most infamous moments of his rule was a fire which had destroyed much of Rome. Nero was accused of having set the fire himself. To shift the blame, Nero blamed the fire on Christians. Nero's conduct came to typify a leader who is inactive and complacent in addressing a serious crisis. This is why Malcolm X had compared John F. Kennedy to Nero because of Kennedy's inaction when it came to dealing with the race problem in America.

Under Nero's rule, the empire experienced rebellions. There was one in Britain which was led by a woman named Boudicca. The Roman towns in London were sacked and as many as 70,000 Romans were killed. There was also a Jewish uprising. Nero was more interested in the arts than in maintaining the military dominance of the empire.

In 65, a plot to overthrow Nero was exposed and the conspirators were executed. This was not the last attempt to remove Nero. In 68, Julius Vindex gained support among the Gauls who were tired of the burden of taxation and debt. Vindex was defeated, but the revolt spread. Galba revolted as well. Realizing that he lacked support, Nero died at the hands of one of his servants, although rumors that Nero was still alive persisted.

The period following Nero's death was one of instability. Galba became the new emperor, but he was murdered. The throne was given to Otho who was then defeated by Vitellius' troops. Vitellius was then overthrown and the throne was given to Flavius

Vespasian. All of this took place within the span of a year.

Nero opposed Christianity, but Christianity eventually spread in Rome and became the dominant religion. In the early years of Christianity in Rome, Christians were viewed as a Jewish sect which strayed from the norms of Judaism. Christianity was also met with hostility from the Roman emperors. Nero executed Christians in Rome after the great fire which he blamed them for. In 303, Diocletian issued decrees which deprived Christians of their rights as citizens and ordered the destruction of their churches. In time, Christianity found acceptance from Constantine who not only restored the civil rights of Christians, but he also built churches.

Christianity came to supplant paganism as the dominant religion in Rome. The Roman emperors themselves began to root out paganism. This created a situation in which followers of the pagan religions were forced to defend their faith. A statesman named Symmachus, who led a movement to restore the altar of Victory which had been removed from the senate house, opposed rigid monotheism which did not allow each to practice their own customs. He stated: "There is no single road by which we may arrive at so great a mystery." In the end, the Christian influence prevailed. Edicts were put in place to confiscate the salaries of pagan priests and to ban sacrifices. Those who were outspoken in their pagan beliefs were excluded from office and from the army.

Prior to the acceptance of Christianity, Roman society had worshiped a supreme sky god known as Jupiter, who was known as Zeus to the Greeks. The story of Zeus was attested in the poems of Homer. Zeus was the leader of all the gods. These gods were to be appeased through rituals and sacrifices. The Greeks also believed that great heroes went to the Elysian fields when they died, whereas most men went to Hades.

The historian John Henrik Clarke argued that Europeans did not have the temperament for Christianity. Erich Fromm made a similar point when he argued that Christianity was at odds with the Greek and Germanic tradition of celebrating great conquerors. Whereas Greek religion told stories of great heroes and conquerors, the story of Jesus was the story of a martyr who sacrificed his life for the benefit of others. It is not as though Greek religion was without examples of martyrs. There was the tale of

Prometheus, who was subjected to a cruel punishment by Zeus for taking fire away from the gods to give it to human beings. This can be viewed as an act of sacrifice because what Prometheus did caused him to be punished even though humanity ultimately benefitted from his action. Generally speaking, however, Greek religious tradition was one which favored heroic conquerors, which is why there was a separate afterlife for heroes as opposed to ordinary people. In Christianity, everyone is equal before God when it comes time for judgment in the afterlife. Those who enter heaven in the Christian religion are not great warriors and heroes, but those who lived a righteous life.

Greco-Roman culture formed the basis of Western civilization, but Western civilization as we know it to be really did not come into being until after the spread of Christianity into Europe. Christianity provided a stronger sense of cultural connection in Europe because it united Europe under a common religion. This religion also helped to set the West apart from the rest of the world. Christianity even became a tool in the process of colonial conquest. Africans were viewed as being heathens who needed to be saved through Christian conversion by the European colonizers.

Theodosius was the last emperor to rule over a unified empire. Theodosius came to power at a time when the Goths were posing a danger to Rome. In 376, Valens permitted the Goths to settle under the protection of the Roman Empire. They were also promised supplies, but this promise was not fulfilled. The Goths, who were facing starvation, began to plunder Rome. When Valens attacked, his army was defeated. Theodosius was made emperor and he managed to subdue the Goths. Theodosius died in 395, leaving two sons who were each given one half of the empire. Arcadius was given the eastern part and Honorius was given the west. The empire remained whole and all edicts were issued in the name of both emperors.

The western portion of the empire eventually collapsed after years of a slow decline. One of the signs of this decline was that "barbarian nations" who were looked down upon by the Romans eventually came to form a major part of the Roman army. Rome found itself being unable to sustain the large empire which it had established. The eastern portion became what is known as the Byzantine Empire. The difference between east and west was as much cultural as it was geographic. The language of administration in the east was Greek, rather than the Latin of the West. The religious doctrines of the two differed as well, with the Orthodox Greek Church having a doctrine which diverged from the Latin Catholics.

The emperor Heraclius managed to defeat Persia and regained control of Syria. The Roman control of Syria was not to last long, however. Sanford noted: "At the very moment of Heraclius' great victory, the first bands of Arabs, inspired by the teachings of Mohammed, the inability of their land to support its growing population, and the ambition of their leaders, began raids which were to result in the conquest of a larger territory than Rome had ever ruled."

The emergence of Islam posed a serious challenge to the dominance of Western civilization. Muslims took control over the regions which were previously under the rule of the Romans. Sanford noted that the Syrians welcomed the Arabs who provided relief from Byzantine oppression. Sanford presented this as a situation in which the "Semites recovered sovereignty in the eastern world [...]." Sanford also noted that by the middle of the eight century the former territories of the Roman Empire were split between the Byzantine Empire with its capital at Constantinople, the Abbasid Caliphate, and the Franks. All three of these powers drew from the Greco-Roman world for their literature and science. Arab scholars translated the works of the Greek philosophers and scientists.

In time, the spread of Islam encroached on Europe itself. In 711, Moors from North Africa seized control of Spain. Muslim rule in Spain was to last several centuries. In 1453, Constantinople fell to the Turks. The conquest of the Ottoman Turks also had a significant impact on trade in Europe because it blocked eastern trade routes.

The period from the fall of the Roman Empire to the 1492 discovery of the Americas was a period of decline and stagnation in Europe. This was a political decline in the sense that Western Europe did not have a state which matched the military might of the Roman Empire of the past. Europe also confronted the threat of

Islamic invasion from the West and from the East. In the West, the Moors managed to seize control of Iberia. In the East, the Byzantine Empire fell to the Turks.

The Roman Empire provided a strong centralized power in Europe. Following the fall of Rome, feudal kingdoms emerged in Europe. Under the feudal system, peasants worked for landlords in exchange for protection. Most of these peasants were serfs who were bound to estates and obligated to serve their landlords. Within this system there was a significant disparity between the wealthy and the poor. The Catholic Church was also an institution which had significant power and authority in Europe at this time.

In a paper titled "The Black Death, an Unforeseen Exchange: Europe's Encounter with Pandemic Sparked an Age of Exploration," Camryn Franke noted that in the centuries prior to the Black Plague, "Europe became prime for a pandemic". The factors which made Europe prime for a pandemic included a massive population increase, urbanization, unsanitary living conditions, and inadequate healthcare. Franke explained: "Many Europeans lived in unsanitary and squalid conditions. People in cities lived in close contact and interacted with disease vectors like rodents and waste." These poor conditions were partly related to the fact that when the Western Roman Empire fell, infrastructure crumbled. Waste ran through the streets due to lack of running water and sewers. Yet another factor which contributed to the plague was the Hundred Years' War between England and France which lasted from 1337 to 1453. During this war, soldiers often encountered disease and returned home to spread it.

In 1347, the plague spread to Eastern Europe. From the east it then spread north and west into Europe. The plague killed millions and led to a collapse in the social order. Entire villages were wiped out by the plague. The plague was especially harmful for the lower class in European society. Giovanni Boccaccio explained that the lower class and most of the middle class received no care and attention, so almost all of them died. It was estimated that one third of the population in Europe perished due to the plague.

The plague also led to significant social changes. As the labor supply declined, peasants realized that they could demand higher wages. In England, King Edward III tried to quell these demands by issuing the Statute of Laborers which required every able-bodied unemployed person under the age of sixty to work for anyone who wanted to hire him. This failed to stop the peasants' demands, however.

Peasant uprisings continued in Europe. Eventually, peasants managed to secure increased wages. This caused serfdom to disappear in many places in Europe. Serfs, who were no longer tied to a landlord, could leave for another who would hire him. The freedom of the workers to leave to find other work resulted in many manors collapsing.

The plague led to the weakening of the feudal system. It also led to a weakening of the Catholic Church's power. After the plague, medical practices improved. More individuals also turned to independent practitioners. Prior to the plague, healthcare was operated by the Catholic Church, but following the plague there was an increase in healthcare options outside of the Catholic Church. Apart from this, the plague also raised questions about the Catholic Church's inability to protect people from the plague. It led to increased mistrust of the Catholic Church, which eventually resulted in religious reformations.

The Black Plague devastated Europe, but it also led to social changes in Europe which weakened the existing feudalistic system. These social changes also contributed to the Renaissance and the age of exploration for Europe. There was an economic transformation as well. As the feudal system weakened, Europe developed mercantilism which was a system based on using exports to increase national wealth. Mercantilism served as the precursor to capitalism.

Sanford pointed out that even after Rome fell, the idea of empire itself persisted. There was a belief that imperial power in the West merely transferred to the Franks when Charlemagne was crowned in 800 and then by Otto the Great in 962, which began the history of the Holy Roman Empire. Constantinople was identified as the Second Rome and Moscow positioned itself as the Third Rome. Sanford noted that even after Napoleon ended the Holy Roman Empire in 1806, the title persisted in central Europe until the 1917 revolution in Russia and the 1918 revolution in Prague.

Greece and Rome also shaped the early formation of the United

States. Greek and Latin were taught in nine Colonial Colleges, which demonstrated how strong the interest in Greece and Rome were in the American colonies. Thomas Jefferson and John Adams admired the achievements of Greece and Rome. Adams believed that Sparta should have been the model for the United States to follow. One of the most obvious points of influence was that the United States adopted the republicanism of Rome.

The importance of understanding the roots of Western civilization and white identity is because these concepts formed the basis of the colonial world order. This is a world order which placed Western civilization at the top, whereas all others were regulated to being colonial subjects who were exploited for the benefit of the dominant colonial power.

The supposed moral and cultural superiority was backed by the technological superiority of the West. It was this technological superiority of the West which allowed the West to conquer and colonize Africa. The technological superiority of the West and its desire for military dominance became a shortcoming during the World Wars. I shan't go into the details about the World Wars other than to state here that the military aggression and rapid advancement in military technology which enabled the Western powers to establish colonial empires around the world eventually resulted in two extremely destructive wars among the European powers which resulted in the deaths of millions. I do not deny the many great achievements of Western civilization, but I do believe they should be weighed against the negative impact as well. For African people, in particular, the impact has been overwhelmingly negative.

2 IN DEFENSE OF THE AFRICAN RACE: THE LEGACY OF ANTÉNOR FIRMIN

Anténor Firmin was a Haitian lawyer, politician, historian, anthropologist, and revolutionary leader. He was a man with many different intellectual interests, but these interests were all utilized for the goal of advancing the African race. Firmin lived at a time when racism was not only enforced in the political policies and agendas of Western nations, but such racism was justified by the theories of anthropologists who argued that white people were the superior race. Firmin refused to accept the notion that black people were an inferior race of people and for this reason he dedicated his life to challenging these racist assertions.

The field of anthropology was one which has produced racist ideas which helped to justify the oppression of African people. One example of this is the Brazilian anthropologist Raimundo Nina Rodrigues who was a noted racist. These racist anthologists used the guise of science to promote the concept of white supremacy and black inferiority. It was this racism that Firmin intended to challenge with his book *On the Equality of Human Races*.[1] Firmin was not the first black man to point to the unity of human races. This was the argument that Martin Delany put forward when he wrote *Principia of Ethnology: The Origin of Races and Color with an Archaeological Compendium of Ethiopia and Egyptian Civilization*. Much like Firmin would later do, Delany cited Egypt and Ethiopia as examples of the capacity for black people to produce great civilizations.

The question is what is race? Race is not a scientific concept. Yet this does not mean that race does not exist as a biological phenomenon. This is to say that physical differences among humans do exist, but such differences alone do not indicate a difference in species. A white man is just as human as a black man. Race does not simply describe a physical difference, but a social difference as well. Thus, race is partly biological and partly social. What this means is that race is a product of a person's ancestry and a product of the social group which a person identifies with.

In some instances, a person's racial identity is based more so on their social identity than their phenotypic appearance. The historian John Henrik Clarke spoke of his colleague John G. Jackson.[2] Jackson was a historian who wrote books on African history, such as *Introduction to African Civilization* and *Ethiopia and the Origin of Civilization*. Clarke explained that Jackson "looked whiter than most white people. He didn't have to walk down the black course. It was a choice, a conscious choice." Jackson consciously chose to identify as black, even though he was not always accepted as such because he did not look black. Clarke explained that in his hometown, Jackson was disrespected by black people who thought Jackson was a white man.

Some Marxists have argued that the working class, regardless of their racial background, have a common interest in joining together to fight against capitalist exploitation. Such a position is not necessarily incorrect, yet, as W.E.B. Du Bois explained in *Dusk of Dawn*, the communist "philosophy did not envisage a situation where instead of a horizontal division of classes, there was a vertical fissure, a complete separation of classes by race, cutting square across the economic layers." Du Bois also explained that "the split between white and black workers was greater than that between white workers and capitalists", which demonstrated the profound influence of race as a factor which shapes social relations.

For people of African descent, the question of race is especially important because race was used as a justification for slavery and colonialism. Race as a construct to divide humanity into different categories is unscientific, yet the impact that the concept of race has had on African people around the world has been very real. The impact of this racism is what Firmin was forced to confront in his day.

That Firmin was from Haiti was also significant to the work that he was engaged in. Haiti was the only nation in the Americas where enslaved Africans were able to successfully overthrow their slave masters to create a republic for themselves. Following this successful revolution, Haiti would struggle to deal with both external and internal pressures. The struggles which Haiti experienced were used by white supremacists as proof of the inferiority of the black race. For this reason, Firmin was especially sensitive to these racist theories.

Firmin was born in Haiti in 1850. As a young man, Firmin worked in different professions including as a teacher and a civil servant. Firmin also studied law and became a lawyer in 1875, at the age of 25. Firmin's early involvement in politics came as a supporter of the Liberal Party. The division between blacks and mulattos in Haitian society was one which went back to the days of the revolution. The division remained prevalent in Haitian society and influenced the politics in Haiti. As such, the National Party was a mostly black party, whereas the Liberal Party was a mostly mulatto party.

The Liberal Party advocated for a strong legislature and civil government rather than military rule. Their slogan was "government by the most competent". Jean Price-Mars[3] stated that Firmin "was already liberal before the formation of the Liberal Party." In support of the Liberal Party, Firmin created a journal called *The Message of the North* in 1878.

Firmin was not a mulatto, but he joined the Liberal Party. Firmin criticized the manner in which division between blacks and mulattos in Haiti was fostered for political purposes. Firmin experienced this himself. He noted that in the 1879 electoral campaign, his political opponents attempted to get the people of the countryside to unite against his candidacy by telling them that Firmin was a mulatto who was as clear-skinned as a white man.[4] Firmin would lose the election which he contested in 1879.

The problem of colorism in Haiti also impacted Firmin's domestic life. Firmin married Marie Louise Rosa Salnave in 1881. Together they had two children. Salnave was the daughter of President Sylvain Salnave. The union between Firmin and Salnave was initially opposed by their parents. There were rumors that the marriage was opposed because Firmin was black and Salnave was a mulatto[5]. Salnave would instead marry Gervais Piquion, but this marriage lasted for two years before Piquion died in 1878. The two did not have children together. Firmin and Rosa married a few years after Rosa's first marriage ended. That Firmin would choose to marry a light-skinned woman seems consistent with Firmin's remarks in *On the Equality of Human Races*, in which he expressed the view that mulattos are more beautiful than black and white people.[6]

Mrs. Firmin was apparently very defensive of her husband. Price-Mars recounted a particular incident which demonstrated this defensive nature.[7] Joseph Cadet Jérémie went to meet Mrs. Firmin. Jérémie recounted that Mrs. Firmin rejected his greeting. Her response was, "after all that you have done to my husband, you dare stretch out your hand to me." After this incident, Boisrond Canal remarked: "A man whose wife is such a woman cannot be President of Haiti." Far from reflecting poorly on Firmin, the incident demonstrated that his wife was very defensive of him and was not quick to forgive Firmin's political opponents. Price-Mars explained that Mrs. Firmin's behavior was that of a woman "who had suffered in her soul, in her heart, in her affection against the injustices and iniquities of which her husband had been the victim."

Firmin developed a relationship with President Lysius Salomon, who appointed Firmin as the sub-inspector of schools for the district of Cap-Haitien. Salomon also appointed Firmin to represent Haiti in Caracas, Venezuela, for an event to commemorate the centenary of the birth of Simon Bolivar. Price-Mars explained that Firmin and Salomon shared the same conception of the unity of the human species and that they both advocated the same objective, which was to "see that Haiti, the eldest daughter of Africa, emerged from slavery by the heroism of her children, should be a model, an example of the perfectibility of the black man and his ability to promote progress in all of the postulates of Western civilization." Where the two men differed was on the question of methods. Even with these differences, Firmin still remained sympathetic to Salomon and agreed to serve in Salomon's government in a non-political capacity. Eventually differences between the two men caused Firmin to sever his contact with Salomon. Firmin left Haiti in 1883 and went to Paris, France.

It was during Firmin's time in Paris that Firmin wrote and published what would become his most influential book, *On the Equality of Human Races*. This book was written as a response to Joseph Arthur de Gobineau's work, which had argued for the inequality of the human races. Gobineau classified humanity into three categories: the Aryans, the Yellows, and the Negroes. Price-Mars described Gobineau's work as "science fiction" which created a stir in Germany. Gobineau's claim that Germans descended from the Aryan race would lay the foundations for the Nazi ideology years later. In his work, Gobineau also used Haiti as an example to support his argument for the inferiority of the black race. He argued that the history of democratic Haiti "is merely a long series of massacres" and that the black race belongs to "a branch of the human family that is incapable of civilization."

Firmin's work challenged this doctrine of racial inequality by asserting the equality of all human races. A major component of Firmin's argument was to explain why it was that the white race came to view itself as being a superior race to others. He wrote in *On the Equality of Human Races* that "the white race dominates everywhere. Proud of its unprecedented position, it must find it natural that all other races accept its laws and obey its will. Why should it be otherwise? It controls science, this science which has become the greatest authority, the least discussed, and the most respectable of those to which one can appeal." Firmin noted that this same science was used to discover and explain secret forces of the universe which seemed to ancients to be supernatural phenomena which were conjured by some invisible entity.

Firmin then praised the white race for producing men such as Newton, Shakespeare, Humboldt, Schiller, and others. Firmin conceded that the white race has every right to be prouder of these men than the Egyptians of all their pyramids and other Pharaonic constructions. Firmin also mentioned engineering wonders such as the building of the Suez Canal in Africa and the Panama Canal in the Americas. He saw the building of the Panama Canal as the physical separation between the Anglo-Saxons of North America and the Latins in South America.

Firmin explained that as Europeans behold their achievements—which he argued were more beautiful than anything that has preceded it—Europeans could be forgiven for believing that they were born to rule the world. Firmin's concern was how to bring Europeans back to reality. He noted that Europeans had not always been so advanced. He also challenged the notion that the black race was an inferior race. To demonstrate this, Firmin pointed to the achievements of black people throughout history.

Rather than challenging the premise of civilization as defined by European writers, Firmin conceded that at the present moment Europeans have a civilization which is more advanced than that which Africans have. Firmin was not wrong in the sense that he did recognize that scientific advancements in Europe resulted in Europeans acquiring a dominant position in the world. It is important to note that the scientific advancements of Europe were often achieved at the expense of Africans and other people who were conquered by Europeans. This was the point which Eric Williams would make in *Capitalism and Slavery* and the point which Walter Rodney would make in *How Europe Underdeveloped Africa*. Firmin's writings did not explore the relationship between Europe's scientific advancement and European colonialism, nor did he address the role of slavery and colonialism in Africa's underdevelopment. Even so, Firmin certainly did recognize that Africa at the time was underdeveloped when compared to Europe and concluded that Europe at the time had a more advanced civilization than Africa's.

Firmin argued that the source of Africa's comparative underdevelopment was the environment. He explained: "Whenever we have to consider the slowness that Africans take to emerge from their present state of inferiority, we must therefore be careful not to believe that this long incapacity is the sign of an organic and fatal inferiority. It will suffice to remember that if the men of the European race, left to their own efforts, deprived of the long experience of a civilization that is many years old and above all of the hereditary culture of a long succession of generations, were condemned to living under the depressive influences of the tropical climate, they could never overcome the difficulties against which black Africans have to struggle."

Firmin did not seek to challenge the idea that Western civilization was the most advanced civilization in the world. Firmin's argument was that the dominance of Europeans was not evidence that Africans and other races were inherently inferior or incapable of achieving what Europeans had achieved. Firmin conceded that Africa at the time was not as advanced as Europe, but he noted that in the past the Africans of Egypt had a more advanced civilization than Europe had and that the civilization of Egypt even influenced the development of Greece. Firmin noted that Thales of Miletus was the first Greek scientist who dealt with mathematics and that he had acquired the best part of his knowledge in Egypt. Firmin also raised the question of whether or not Pythagoras arrived at his ideas through Egyptian priests after studying under them in Thebes.

George M. James would also explore the idea that the Greeks owe the development of their civilization to Africans in a book titled *Stolen Legacy*. James argued that Greek philosophy was the product of the Egyptian mystery system. To support this argument, James pointed out that philosophers in Athens were treated very poorly: "Another point of considerable interest to be accounted for was the attitude of the Athenian government towards this so-called Greek philosophy, which it regarded as foreign in origin and treated it accordingly. Only a brief study of history is necessary to show that Greek philosophers were undesirable citizens, who throughout the period of their investigations were victims of relentless persecution, at the hands of the Athenian government. Anaxagoras was imprisoned and exiled; Socrates was executed; Plato was sold into slavery and Aristotle was indicted and exiled; while the earliest of them all, Pythagoras, was expelled from Croton in Italy." Years before James published *Stolen Legacy*, Firmin would declare that the black race was the oldest of all other races in the career of civilization and that white people who spoke of the inferiority of blacks were merely "ingrates".

Firmin maintained that Pharaonic Egypt was a black civilization. The racial identity of the ancient Egyptians is a topic which has been contested by scholars. Price-Mars himself concluded that "it would be somewhat risky to claim that the population of ancient Egypt was completely black or even Negroid. We would be much closer to reality by maintaining that it was, in large part, mixed race and that its mixing revealed a considerable contribution from black Africa." In Firmin's view, there was little doubt as to the racial identity of the ancient Egyptians.

Another topic which Firmin confronted in his book were the theories of Clémence Royer. Royer translated Darwin's *Origin of*

Species into French. In Royer's view, Darwin's work supported the notion of racial inequality. She argued that the theory of natural selection was one which left no doubt that superior races emerge and that these superior races are destined to supplant the inferior races. Royer also believed that racial mixing had the effect of lowering the average level of the species. Royer's views on race can be demonstrated by an encounter she had with Firmin. Royer and Firmin were both members of the Paris Anthropology Society. On one occasion when Firmin challenged the racist theories being promoted by some of the members, Royer confronted Firmin and asked him if his intellectual ability was not the result of some white ancestry.[8]

In his response to Royer in *On the Equality of Human Races*, Firmin noted the fact that she was a woman. In his view only men have the education and temperament to study complex issues from all sides. Here, Firmin employed sexism as a response to Royer's ideas by suggesting that a woman would not be capable of fully understanding Darwin's theory. In a book which argued for the equality of races, it would appear that Firmin also suggested an inequality among the sexes. Firmin does not elaborate more on this point, so one is not sure if Firmin believed that these differences between men and women are biological, or if he is referring to the social conditioning of women. Whatever the case may have been, this remark by Firmin certainly stands out because it seems rather at odds with Firmin's mission of challenging unscientific ideas.

Firmin also challenged the notion that the white race had greater morality than the black race. Firmin explained that prostitution was so well-accepted in Greek and Roman antiquity that "it is impossible to understand how such institutions could coexist with the refinements of civilizations who tolerated them." Firmin also noted that such acts of immorality still persist in Europe. He noted that in certain large European cities, "acts of revolting immorality take place in the open air."

Aside from pointing to sexual immorality among the white race, Firmin also wrote about the behavior of the white race to other races of the world. He explained: "As for the relations of Europeans with men of another race, especially with blacks, there is nothing more dreadful, nothing more barbarous. The whole history of the slave trade is stained with bloody pages, where crimes of all kinds occur with such frequency that one would have to say that the owners of slaves were prey to cruel madness." This passage is important because the racism of white people was precisely the reason why it was necessary for Firmin to write *On the Equality of Human Races*.

Firmin presented the struggles and achievements of African people in the face of such racism as further evidence of the capacity of the black race. He particularly cited Toussaint Louverture, who was one of the leaders of the Haitian Revolution. Of Toussaint, Firmin wrote: "It echoes in my heart and comforts my faith in the future of my race, of the black race whose incomparable, eternal glory, is to have produced such a man, where so many other races would have offered only a brute with a human face." Toussaint was born a slave, but he overcame those conditions to become a brilliant revolutionary leader. Toussaint represented the ability of the black race to produce great leaders under adverse conditions, which is why Firmin wrote: "Certainly, when a race has produced an individuality as marvelously gifted as Toussaint-Louverture was, it is impossible to admit that it is inferior to others, without demonstrating an inconceivable blindness or absence of logic."

In Firmin's view, the black race would come to pursue justice more forcibly than other races have done. He wrote: "Splendid will be the role it will have to play in the world. Its great share of action, in the blossoming of progress, will be above all to develop the sense of justice with much more force and, at the same time, much more of delicacy than the jaded and dry-hearted races which arose in Europe or which grew in the plains of the Middle Kingdom and Tartary." In expressing this view, Firmin is not necessarily asserting that black people inherently have a superior morality to other races. Firmin expressed the view that the "races are equal; they are all capable of achieving the noblest intellectual development, as they are of falling into the most complete degradation." Firmin also noted that the Egyptians enslaved other races, including the children of Seth and Japheth—this was a reference to the Biblical enslavement of the Hebrews in Egypt. Firmin mentioned this to show that there was a period in time when black people had enslaved other races. The point that he made was that all races had been guilty of oppressing other races at some point in their history.

Firmin's treatment of religion in *On the Equality of Human Races* is interesting because it relates to a topic in Haitian history which Firmin would address in a later work. Firmin saw in Haiti's history a conflict between modernization and traditional African superstitions. In *Mr. Roosevelt, President of the United States and the Republic of Haiti*, he explained that Henri Christophe followed Toussaint and Jean-Jacques Dessalines in employing his energy to combat African superstitions. Firmin argued that Alexandre Pétion had taken the opposite view of Toussaint, Dessalines, and Christophe. Firmin explained that under Pétion's rule, those who wanted to be free abandoned cultivated land and lived in the woods where they were pushed back to ancestral savagery. Firmin does not elaborate on either of these points to define what he meant by African superstitions and ancestral savagery, but one could conclude that Firmin is referring to traditional African religious practices such as voodoo.[9]

Firmin's view of religion was that religions were superstitious beliefs which would lose their relevance as science progressed. In *On the Equality of Human Races*, Firmin wrote: "A fact that cannot be concealed is the serene indifference that all men of high intelligence, in all times and in all civilizations, have always shown towards religious practices." Firmin also expressed the view that "faith is dying." He noted that an increasing number of individuals were turning away from Christianity, though Firmin also recognized that the transition away from Christianity is not an easy one for white people. Firmin made the argument that it would be easier for black people to transition away from religion. He explained: "Never having conceived the religious fanaticism and the dogmatic spirit, in the shackles of which the Caucasian race painfully struggles, the Blacks find themselves quite ready to evolve towards rational and positive conceptions, in conformity with the system of the universe and the resulting moral order."

Firmin described African religions as being "fetishism and totemism" which he described as being the adoration of animals and stones, as well as the belief in charms accompanied by repugnant and bloodthirsty rites. Firmin did note that these practices are also found among several backward nations of other races. He explained that all the peoples of the white race also had a period in their existence in which they practiced fetishism, so that this practice is not limited only to African people alone.

Firmin is not totally dismissive of African religions for he also argued that the religion of African people was not wholly based on superstitious rituals. He described African religions as "a kind of practical rationalism" in which Africans believed that the greater deity is so far above humans that it is too great to worry about human affairs. Firmin made reference to Mungo Park's observation that the Mandinka people believe that God is so superior that they believe it was ridiculous to imagine that mortals could change the decrees or the aim of infallible wisdom through prayer.

Firmin rejected the notion that humanity can be divided into a racial hierarchy in which whites were the superior race, but he did not completely reject the concept of race itself. This may seem like a contradictory position, but Firmin understood that although race did not exist as a scientific reality, the social reality of race was real and had an effect on the lives of African people. Thus, by bringing attention to the achievements of great African civilizations and great individual leaders such as Toussaint, Firmin was demonstrating that African people were just as capable of contributing to human civilization as other races.

Firmin was also a Pan-Africanist who believed that Haiti had a role to play in the rehabilitation of Africa.[10] Not only did Firmin believe that Haiti had to serve in the rehabilitation of Africa, but he believed that the elevation of the black race would help Haiti. Firmin wrote in the preface to *Mr. Roosevelt:* "As long as black people continue to be an object of contempt by other men, whether white or yellow, Haiti will never be taken seriously…" Firmin recognized that the destiny of Haiti was linked to the destiny of other African people around the world. He demonstrated this link in *On the Equality of Human Races*, where he explained that the independence of Haiti "had a positive influence on the fate of the whole Ethiopian race, living outside Africa."

For Firmin, the question of unity is significant for

understanding the European conquest of the world. In *On the Equality of Human Races*, Firmin expressed the observation that all the European nations, of the white race, are naturally inclined to unite in order to dominate the rest of the world and that "whenever a European power lends its ostensible or hidden assistance to a people of Asia or Africa, it is to better paralyze the progress of a rival, whose greatness it is jealous of or fears, than to favor this people to whom it comes to aid only with the ulterior motive of being able to exploit it in turn." Firmin also noted that the focus of European politics seemed to be Asia and Africa. He particularly focused on the European presence in Africa, where he noted that Europeans justified their colonial conquests on the basis that Europeans have a right to exterminate those who resist their invasion.

Whereas Europeans have been united in their efforts to conquer the world, Africans have had to face the challenge of disunity. This was particularly the case for Haiti. In *Mr. Roosevelt*, Firmin noted that the diversity of ethnic groups was one of the challenges which Haiti had to confront given that the Africans in Haiti were drawn from different parts of Africa and came from different ethnic groups. Firmin wrote that Haiti was populated by "strangers forced together from diverse places in Africa, often as distant as the space that extends from Portugal to the Ural Mountains..." Firmin continued to note that these Africans spoke very diverse languages, which was unlike European languages which have a common Latin influence and therefore share some words in common. Firmin argued that the invasion of Arabs improved the state of affairs by providing an Africanized language of the conquerors, but that the difficulty in understanding each other still remained an obstacle for Africans.

Firmin attended the Pan-African Conference in 1900 which was held in London. Carolyn Fluehr-Lobban explained: "Had he not been preoccupied with Haitian politics and a bid to become President as head of a Firminist movement, ending in his exile in St Thomas ordered by President Nord Alexis, Firmin might have continued to be involved on an international level with the nascent Pan-Africanist movement." Indeed, it would seem that Firmin's primary concern was Haitian politics. Firmin's view was that Haiti had to serve in the rehabilitation of Africa. It is not apparent what Firmin had in mind when he wrote this statement, however. One is not sure how Firmin envisioned Haiti assisting with the rehabilitation of Africa. What is apparent from this remark by Firmin is that he was concerned with the rehabilitation of Africa and believed that Haiti should play a role in this process.

Henry Sylvester Williams, who organized the Pan African Conference, did not conceptualize the Pan-African movement as an anti-colonial movement to liberate Africa from colonial domination. In Williams' view, the Pan-African movement was one which would secure the rights and business interests of Africans living in "civilized" countries of the world.[11] Firmin's view on this issue is difficult to ascertain. Firmin invoked Africa's ancient past to counter the claims of black inferiority, but he wrote very little about the contemporary situation in Africa. Fluehr-Lobban noted that "Firmin was largely ignorant of the contemporary African continent of his day, recalling that much of the African interior had yet to be fully explored and mapped at the time of the writing of *De l'égalité des races humaines*, in 1885. The Berlin Congress dividing the continent amongst the major European powers had occurred the year before, in 1884." The colonial powers of Europe partitioned Africa among themselves. By 1900, Africa had been colonized by various European nations. Firmin certainly recognized that this desire for global conquest on the part of Europeans was detrimental to the people of Africa, but it would appear that Firmin was more concerned with strengthening and protecting Haiti than with confronting colonialism in Africa.

Price-Mars, who was influenced by Firmin's work, expanded on the Pan-African work of Firmin. Firmin challenged racist theories about African people, but he seemed largely indifferent towards affirming the African cultural roots of the people of Haiti. Price-Mars, on the other hand, explored the African roots of Haitian culture in more depth than Firmin seemed interested in doing. Price-Mars also went further than Firmin in challenging the manner in which the colonial legacy shaped the way that Haitians viewed their own identity. In his book *So Spoke the Uncle*, Price-Mars noted that some Haitians disassociated from their African ancestry and preferred to view themselves as colored Frenchman.[12] Massillion Coicou, a poet who was killed for his role in the Firminist rebellion, went so far as to write a poem in which he professed his love of France and expressed the view that Haiti was the "Black France."[13] This was an example of the type of mentality which Price-Mars referred to.

This type of thinking displayed that although Haiti was politically independent, many Haitians were still psychologically colonized. This psychological colonization led some Haitians to recoil from their African identity and seek to embrace the identity of the colonizer. It would appear that Firmin was proud of his African identity and did not view himself as a black Frenchman, although he did express the view that Haiti shared a common destiny with France. In *Mr. Roosevelt*, Firmin explained that Haitians had a tie of sympathy to France which could not be erased "from the heart of the Haitians, without erasing all the pages of our history, which prove that, even while fighting each other, in the great struggle for freedom and national independence, Haitians and French kept something in common, the generosity of the heart and the admiration of true courage wherever it comes from."

Firmin explained: "By language, Haiti is France..." He continued to note that although Haiti was proud of its political independence, Haiti was also proud of the ties that bind it to "the old mother country" and seeks to strengthen those ties by imitating whatever comes to Haiti from France. Firmin did not seem to question this connection to France in the way that Price-Mars would later do. In Firmin's view, the duty of France was to cooperate with the United States to help Haiti rise more and more in the ways of civilization.

At first glance, there seems to be a significant gap between the work of Price-Mars and Firmin. After all, whereas Price-Mars openly challenged Haiti's psychological attachment to France and pointed to Haiti's African roots, Firmin seemed to have unquestionably accepted the fact that Haiti remained culturally connected to France, despite having won its political independence from France through a bloody revolution. Where Firmin differs compared to some other Haitian intellectuals was that Firmin did not seek to disassociate himself from Africa. Firmin had declared in *On the Equality of Human Races* that there was no fundamental difference between the blacks of Africa and the blacks of Haiti. This alone was a profound remark which displayed Firmin's Pan-African worldview and his embrace of Africa.

France of Firmin's day was one of the colonial powers which was exploiting the people of Africa through colonialism. One would have hardly expected France to have done anything to contribute to Haiti's development, but Firmin was optimistic about the possibility that France and the United States would assist Haiti. Haiti's relationship to France, as Firmin pointed out, was based on a shared history and shared language, whereas Firmin saw Haiti's relationship to the United States as being based on a shared history of revolutionary struggle against the colonial forces of Europe.

One could argue that Firmin was perhaps too optimistic in viewing France and the United States as being nations which would serve to uplift Haiti, but Firmin was not alone in his optimism about France and the United States. Marcus Garvey had expressed a similar view. When Garvey noticed France's alarmed reaction to the work that his organization was doing in Africa, Garvey explained: "Why France should act in this manner I am unable to say, because it has always been the belief of a large number of us that France was friendly disposed toward the higher development of the Negro race, but recent happenings have proved to us that France is no better than the other colonial powers that have ravished and exploited Africa for hundreds of years." Regarding the American government, Garvey explained: "We believe that America's friendship for the Negro is unparalleled and that when the time comes America will do more for us as a race than any other government in the world." The American government, just like the French government, was alarmed by Garvey's work and endeavored to oppose what Garvey was doing.[14]

In *Mr. Roosevelt*, Firmin described George Washington as an "illustrious hero" in the War of Independence and as a man whose "immortal name" will always awaken respect and admiration. Despite his praise for the American Revolution, Firmin recognized that the United States was a nation which had not lived up to its ideals. Firmin was particularly concerned about racism in the

United States. He argued that before the American people could assume the role of vanguard of the civilized nations, it must address the problem of Afro-Americans, "whose admission to citizenship and social equality is so hotly contested throughout the American South." Firmin explained that the "question of race or color prejudice" was also a topic of interest for Haitians in their relations with the United States.

Firmin's political vision was hemispheric. He was an early proponent of creating an Antillean confederation years before the formation of the short-lived West Indies Federation or the Caribbean Community (CARICOM). Firmin's interest in Caribbean unity led him to connect with a Puerto Rican nationalist named Ramón Emeterio Betances. Betances also advocated for the creation of a Caribbean federation as well. Firmin not only advocated for a unity of Caribbean nations, but he also believed that the United States and Haiti should form a partnership. Firmin recognized that the two nations shared a similar history, since both nations were born out of a revolutionary struggle against a colonial power from Europe. Firmin put forward this vision in *Mr. Roosevelt*.

That Firmin did not look to Africa as a potential political force for Haiti to align itself with is hardly surprising. Not only was Africa colonized, but, as noted before, Firmin's understanding of Africa was very limited. Firmin had never traveled to Africa, although Benito Sylvain, another Haitian Pan-Africanist who attended the 1900 Pan-African Conference, had traveled to Ethiopia where he met Menelik II. It would appear that Firmin's vision was one in which Haiti would become a strong and stable nation with the support of the United States and France, and then Haiti would work toward establishing a great civilization in Africa. Firmin did not write much about the topic of colonialism in Africa, so it is difficult to determine if Firmin recognized that there would eventually be a struggle against the colonial powers in Europe over Africa's liberation. Firmin certainly condemned the brutal methods which European nations had employed in Africa, but Firmin's immediate concern was the possibility that Haiti could once again be dominated by foreign forces.

In *Mr. Roosevelt*, Firmin addressed the Monroe Doctrine. Firmin expressed support for the Monroe Doctrine, even going so far as to quote the words of the President of the United States, who declared: "I believe with all my soul, in the Monroe Doctrine." Firmin did not oppose the Monroe Doctrine in theory, but he did take issue to the Monroe Doctrine being used to justify American imperialism in the Caribbean. He criticized the American intervention in Cuba under President McKinley. Firmin wrote that McKinley "must have sensed that it was indeed him, the loyal knight, the Lohengrin, protector of the weak, whom the poet called to the help of desperate Cuba."

A French economist named Pierre Leroy-Beaulieu argued that the United States had a right to expand itself by intervening in Haiti, since the "semi-barbarous individuals" do not have the right to prevent the development of their countries "by other countries more civilized than them." Firmin suggested that France should not listen to Leroy-Beaulieu's views. Firmin also questioned why an American president would attempt to seize Haiti given the costs that would be involved in such an endeavor. He wrote: "Besides, what American statesman, shrewd and wise, would want to undertake to seize Haitian territory or a part of it by force, by comparing the benefit of such an acquisition with the efforts and the considerable thoughts, in human lives and in money, that it would be necessary to deploy and carry out to bring its enterprise to a successful conclusion?" Firmin further noted that if Haiti's republic was threatened, Haiti should be determined to fight to preserve its independence. Firmin recognized the need for Haiti to defend itself, although he did not view President Theodore Roosevelt as a threat to Haiti's independence. He believed that Haiti had nothing to fear from Roosevelt. Firmin was correct as Roosevelt was not the president who would oversee the American invasion of Haiti in 1915.

America's imperial intentions towards Haiti became apparent in the affair over Môle St. Nicholas. The United States sought to secure control of Môle St. Nicholas to establish a naval base in the Caribbean. The talks over this territory began in 1981. Frederick Douglass, who at the time was the American ambassador to Haiti, was sent to engage in negotiations. Price-Mars described Firmin as being trapped between Haitian public opinion and American public opinion. In the end, Firmin succeeded in staving off the American claims to Haitian land by citing the Haitian Constitution, which forbade cession of territory to foreigners. Firmin and Douglass both resigned from their positions at the end of the negotiations.[15] Price-Mars explained that from this resounding victory the ideology of "Firminism" was born. He compared Firminism to a religion which had its fanatics and its martyrs. Among those martyrs was the poet, Coicou.[16]

Firminism in Haiti developed into a revolutionary political movement which sought to transform Haiti. Throughout Firmin's life, he had been at the forefront of efforts to politically transform Haiti. When Firmin returned to Haiti in 1888, he joined a revolutionary committee which was organized against Salomon's government. This revolutionary movement managed to successfully remove Salomon from power and a provisional government was established. The provisional government drafted a new constitution for Haiti. Firmin and another lawyer named Léger Cauvin led the debates of the assembly over this new constitution. In the newly established government, Firmin was to serve as the Secretary of State for External Relations, Finance, and Trade. Firmin proved to be very effective at managing the nation's finances. In a short time, the credit of the state was enhanced and there was a gradual rise in the rating of the bonds of external debt on the Paris Stock Exchange.[17]

After another period of being overseas, Firmin returned to Haiti in 1902 to bury the remains of his daughter who died while they were living in France.[18] Now back in Haiti, Firmin decided to struggle against General Nord Alexis for power in Haiti. Alexis and Firmin worked together on the revolutionary committee which had overthrown President Salomon. Now the two men would become bitter political rivals. The wedge between the two men was partly due to the fact that when a new government was formed in 1902, Alexis was included in the government, but Firmin was excluded.[19] Alexis used his position in the new government to position himself into power, while also targeting Firmin and Firmin's supporters.

The contest for power between Firmin and Alexis became a

violent one. Firmin, who had opposed the militarism in Haiti, found himself in a situation where armed struggle was necessary to achieve his political aims in Haiti. In this struggle, Firmin relied on the services of his brother-in-law, Albert Salnave. Salnave and Alexis seemed to have held each other in high esteem. Price-Mars recalled that in 1903 he was brought to the National Palace where he met with Alexis. Papillion was at the meeting as well. Papillion was a former minister who was given the right to return from exile. Alexis asked Papillion about Albert Salnave's life in exile to which Papillion provided some information. Alexis responded by accusing Firmin of having involved his brother-in-law in the rebellion.[20]

Price-Mars attributed Firmin's defeat to Firmin's mistaken decision to order a man named Hammerton Killick to seize arms and ammunition from a German steamer. Rather than allowing his ship, the *Crête-à-Pierrot*, to be captured, Killick decided to destroy the ship. Killick went down along with the ship. Firmin praised Killick's actions, describing his conduct as being glorious. He compared Killick's sacrifice to that of Marcus Curtius of Rome and Louis Delgrès from Martinique. In his statement praising Killick, Firmin instructs Killick as follows:

> You say to Dessalines that contrary to his advice we have admitted the foreigner among us and that he has become the working machine of our troubles and our divisions.
>
> You will tell Christophe that certain Haitians have intentionally kept the people in ignorance, idleness, laziness, but that the descendants of the titans of 1804 are not yet prepared for slavery.[21]

Firmin ended the letter by declaring, "for God, save the black race, save the country, save Haiti." In Firmin's view, Killick had made a great sacrifice in defense of Haiti and the black race, but Price-Mars argued that this incident displayed Firmin's greatest weakness. Price-Mars noted that the decision to seize weapons from a German steamer was a poor one on the part of Firmin and that no one around Firmin was able to advise him properly. Price-Mars explained "Firmin's fault has been attributed to his infatuation. It seems that he had no one in his entourage who had enough authority to make him see to what calamity his decision was going to bring him."

Following his defeat, Firmin went into exile. Firmin continued his resistance to Alexis' government. In 1908, Firmin traveled to the United States, where he declared that with the support of the "sympathetic neutrality" of the American government, he would proceed to overturn Alexis' government in Haiti. A report on this comment by the *New York Times* noted that Firmin was known in diplomatic circles as "a professional revolutionist."[22] The United States expressed little interest in aiding Firmin. As the report noted, Firmin's opposition to granting America a naval base in Haiti was enough to prevent the existence of any kind of sympathy for Firmin. Alexis' government was not viewed as being an ideal government. Alexis faced pressure from the United States after he executed political prisoners, but America had no interest in intervening to help Firmin into power. America was more interested in maintaining Alexis' government in power. Alexis claimed to be pro-American and received American assistance in suppressing the Firminist rebellion in Haiti.[23] Alexis remained president of Haiti until 1908 when he was ousted from power. He left for Jamaica where he lived in exile.

Firmin sought America's help in his endeavor, but he was under no illusion about the fact that Haiti needed to be in control of its own destiny. In *Mr. Roosevelt*, Firmin concluded that even if France were to unite with the American Union to aid Haiti, it would be in vain if Haitians do not decide to take a retrospective look at their past and change their habits. He explained: "Our destiny, in the final analysis, must be our own work."

Firmin spent the last years of his life in exile. Firmin made an attempt to return to Haiti in 1911. He arrived on August 12, but was not allowed to get off the boat. Firmin's presence in Haiti remained a source of concern for the Haitian government. Firmin was allowed to greet friends who wished to see him aboard the steamer, however. After this brief return to Haiti, Firmin returned to St. Thomas, this time accompanied by his wife. Firmin initially went into exile to St. Thomas without his wife. Firmin had attempted to bring his wife with him to St. Thomas. He asked

Captain Le Breton to ask the president for a passport to be issued to Rosa Firmin. The request was granted by President Antoine Simon, but this recommendation was ignored. Firmin, who was ailing, died that same year.[24]

Firmin recalled that America's decision to annex Puerto Rico was "like a fatal blow, aimed at the heart of Doctor Betances, with the irremediable failure of his long-cherished and patriotic hopes." Betances had lived in exile for almost thirty years. He swore to never set foot in Puerto Rico unless it was a free and independent nation, but he watched helplessly as his homeland passed from Spanish domination to American domination. Firmin explained that Betances was more wounded by the overthrow of his aspirations than he was by the disease from which he was suffering from at the time.[25] Firmin would not live to see Haiti suffer a similar fate, although he foretold that such a fate could be possible for Haiti. In the years following Firmin's death, his concerns would prove to be prophetic. Haiti did in fact fall under the foreign domination of the United States in 1915, only four years after Firmin's death.

Since Haiti became independent, Haiti struggled with political stability and military rule. Firmin pointed out in *Mr. Roosevelt* that the danger of national independence obtained by war is that power is concentrated in the hands of the military force, which is both an instrument of coercion and defense.[26] This was precisely the problem in Haiti. The American invasion of Haiti did little to resolve this problem of political instability in Haiti, however. Price-Mars noted that the tradition of having military men in power in Haiti ended following the 1915 invasion of Haiti, but the civilians who came to power were often inferior to their predecessors.[27]

The American occupation of Haiti lasted from 1915 until 1934, but America would continue to influence Haiti's politics even after the occupation ended. The corruption, abuse of power, and instability would continue as well. Firmin's hope and vision for Haiti was that Haiti would serve as a testament for the capability of the African race. This was not a vision which Firmin lived to see, but in the years that followed his passing, Firmin's vision remained just as relevant.

Notes:

1. *De l'égalité des races humaines* (*On the Equality of Human Races*) is one of the two books by Firmin which are referenced in this essay and translated from the original French text. The other book is *M. Roosevelt, Président des États-Unis et la République d'Haïti* (*Mr. Roosevelt, President of the United States and the Republic of Haiti*).

2. John Henrik Clarke's discussion on John G. Jackson here is quoted from "On My Journey Now: The Narrative and Works of Dr. John Henrik Clarke, the Knowledge Revolutionary" in *The Journal of Pan African Studies*, vol. 6, no. 7, February 2014.

3. Jean Price-Mars published a biography of Anténor Firmin titled *Antenor Firmin*. The quotes presented in this essay were translated into English from the original French version.

4. This incident is mentioned by Firmin in *Mr. Roosevelt*. Price-Mars mentioned it as well in *Antenor Firmin*.

5. The rumors surrounding the reason why Firmin was initially rejected when he expressed an interest in marrying Rosa Salnave is addressed by Price-Mars in chapter twelve of his biography.

6. In chapter seven of *On the Equality of Human Races*, Firmin compares physical beauty among the races. He concluded that the color of the white race enhances its beauty more than the Ethiopian race, but he also explained that he found the mulatto to be the most beautiful color of all.

7. This incident is recounted in chapter thirty-seven of Price-Mars' biography on Firmin. Price-Mars explained that it was unclear whether Firmin himself was aware of this incident or what his views on it were if he was aware.

8. This exchange between Firmin and Royer is mentioned by Carolyn Fluehr-Lobban in "Anténor Firmin and Haiti's contribution to anthropology" in *Gradhiva* 1, 2005.

9. Based on the remarks which Firmin made on religion in *On the Equality of Human Races* and in *Mr. Roosevelt*, it would seem that Firmin was not religious, but his writings would suggest that he was not an atheist either.

10. Firmin writes this in the preface of *On the Equality of Human*

Races.

11. For more information on Henry Sylvester Williams' role in the Pan-African movement see "The Historical Aspects of Pan-Africanism: A Personal Chronicle" by Rayford W. Logan.

12. Price-Mars addressed the negative attitude that Haitians had towards their African roots in the preface of *So Spoke the Uncle.*

13. This is a reference to a poem by Massillon Coicou titled "A Un Frainçais" from a collection of Coicou's poems titled *Poésies Nationales.*

14. These quotes by Marcus Garvey are taken from *Selected Writings and Speeches of Marcus Garvey.*

15. Price-Mars provided a detailed account of the negotiations over Môle St. Nicholas in his biography of Firmin. Amy Reinsel also provides a brief summary of the incident in "Poetry of Revolution: Romanticism and National Projects in Nineteenth-century Haiti."

16. Coicou was killed for his role in participating in a Firminist rebellion in Haiti. Coicou's support of the Firminist movement and his execution are detailed by Reinsel in "Poetry of Revolution: Romanticism and National Projects in Nineteenth-century Haiti."

17. Price-Mars detailed Firmin's role in the government in his biography on Firmin.

18. The death of Firmin's daughter Anna is mentioned by Price-Mars in *Antenor Firmin.* Price-Mars explained that Firmin returned to Haiti to bury his daughter in 1902 to dismiss some claims which stated that Firmin returned to Haiti that year to disrupt the general elections. Price-Mars also recounted that in 1901, he was invited to have lunch with Firmin, his wife, and his daughter Anna. Price-Mars wrote: "It was the only time I had the opportunity to see a modest Firmin, mute with admiration, in a conversation in which his daughter displayed the liveliness and grace of her mind." Price-Mars had a lively dialogue with her about the difficulties of the German language and the English language. Anna died a year later.

19. Reinsel provided an account of the conflict between Firmin and Alexis in "Poetry of Revolution: Romanticism and National Projects in Nineteenth-century Haiti." In this account, Reinsel mistakenly stated that General Tiresias Augustin Simon Sam became the president of Haiti in 1902. Sam actually left the office of the presidency in 1902.

20. This is mentioned in Price-Mars' biography. In 1903, Price-

Mars had returned from Europe and was brought to the National Palace by the Minister of War to present his duties to Nord Alexis. Price-Mars concluded that Alexis and Albert Salnave had equal consideration for each other.

21. This statement by Firmin is quoted by Price-Mars in chapter thirty-five of his biography in Firmin. Price-Mars described Firmin as a "fierce doctrinaire" who opposed the domination of class and money oligarchies in Haiti.

22. This was reported in a *New York Times* article from June 22, 1908, titled "Ridicule Firmin's Boasts: State Officials Regard Haitian as a Professional Revolutionist."

23. In "Poetry of Revolution: Romanticism and National Projects in Nineteenth-century Haiti," Reinsel mentioned that in 1908, the United States intercepted an arms' shipment which was headed to Firmin supporters in Haiti.

24. In "Anténor Firmin and Haiti's contribution to anthropology," Fluehr-Lobban states that Firmin was 61 at the time of his death, whereas Price-Mars states that Firmin's age was 60.

25. Firmin's friendship with Doctor Betances and Firmin's views on Caribbean unity are addressed in Firmin's essay titled "Haiti and the Confederation of the Antilles" in *Inter America*, Volume 5.

26. Firmin addressed this topic in the section of *Mr. Roosevelt* which addressed the Haitian government during the reign of Jean-Jacques Dessalines.

27. Price-Mars addressed the American invasion of Haiti in chapter seventeen of his biography on Firmin.

3 A REVIEW OF STATE OF EMERGENCY

President Donald Trump spoke in Poland recently. There he expressed the idea of Western civilization being under threat. President Trump said:

"We urge Russia to cease its destabilizing activities in Ukraine and elsewhere, and its support for hostile regimes—including Syria and Iran—and to instead join the community of responsible nations in our fight against common enemies and in defense of civilization itself.

Finally, on both sides of the Atlantic, our citizens are confronted by yet another danger—one firmly within our control. This danger is invisible to some but familiar to the Poles: the steady creep of government bureaucracy that drains the vitality and wealth of the people. The West became great not because of paperwork and regulations but because people were allowed to chase their dreams and pursue their destinies."

Trump also went on to say in this speech: "The fundamental question of our time is whether the West has the will to survive. Do we have the confidence in our values to defend them at any cost? Do we have enough respect for our citizens to protect our borders? Do we have the desire and the courage to preserve our civilization in the face of those who would subvert and destroy it?" This speech played on the idea of Western civilization being under a threat and needing to defend itself. An aspect of Western civilization's fragility is the ever present need to defend itself, whether it is militarily or morally.

With Trump's remarks as the backdrop, I want to undertake this review of Buchanan's book, *State of Emergency: The Third World Invasion and Conquest*, because of the fact that so many of the views which Trump expressed in his speech in Poland were ideas that were being put forward by Buchanan years prior. Not only did Buchanan write about the need to protect America's borders, but Buchanan also wrote about this threat that Western civilization was facing and the need to defend the West from this threat.

The title of the book is meant to cause alarm and panic at this supposed Third World invasion. The concept of Third World is a very vaguely defined concept. It is most often used to describe poor and developing nations, but what the concept originally referred to were nations that were non-aligned in the Cold War. First World countries were the ones on the side of capitalist America and Second World countries were sided with the Soviet Union. I point this out because Buchanan himself never really defines what he means when he says Third World, although the implication he gives in this text is that he is referring to non-white people.

I think reviewing this book is also important because it demonstrates that Trump's ideas were not new. For some, Trump appears to be a sort of anomaly in politics, but I would make the case that Trump's ideas are actually deeply rooted in Western political tradition. It is for this reason that I do not try to link Trump's campaign to fascism or Nazism because elements of that type of thinking existed in America long before Adolf Hitler thought about them, so I do not believe that we have to necessarily look to Hitler to find the roots of Trump's political thought.

As far as African people are concerned the entire Western system is a fascist one. We were oppressed by the Germans, the Italians, and the Spanish, as well as the Americans, the British, and the French. I want to make this point very clear; the American system has always been a very racist and oppressive one since its founding, so I do not look to Nazi Germany to find the roots of Trump's political ideas. I look right here at America's history.

In *How Europe Underdeveloped Africa*, Walter Rodney argued that the Holocaust was merely a case of Western society's unchecked racism turning inwardly on itself. Rodney explained:

"In the short run, European racism seemed to have done Europeans no harm, and they used those erroneous ideas to justify their further domination of non-European peoples in the colonial epoch. But the international proliferation of bigoted and unscientific racist ideas was bound to have its negative consequences in the long run. When Europeans put millions of their brothers (Jews) into ovens under the Nazis, the chickens were coming home to roost. Such behaviour inside of 'democratic' Europe was not as strange as it is sometimes made out to be. There was always a contradiction between the elaboration of democratic ideas inside Europe and the elaboration of authoritarian and thuggish practices by Europeans with respect to Africans. When the French Revolution was made in the name of 'Liberty, Equality and Fraternity,' it did not extend to black Africans who were enslaved by France in the West Indies and the Indian Ocean. Indeed, France fought against the efforts of those people to emancipate themselves, and the leaders of their bourgeois revolution said plainly that they did not make it on behalf of black humanity."

The reality is that the message of the Nazis was nothing new. That element of racial superiority has existed in Western thought for a very long time. I don't want readers to be under the impression that we are seeing a resurgence of some sort of "neo-fascist" tendency in American politics or in the West. That element was there from the foundation of the country and it is deeply rooted in Western tradition. The Nazi preoccupation with eugenics and racial superiority was always an element of American society; a society which outlawed interracial relations, and which marginalized mixed race individuals to reinforce this racial caste system. A racial caste system developed throughout the Americas.

Nazi Germany and the United States both shared the common belief that Europeans were a superior race. This was demonstrated during World War II. In *Black Power*, Stokely Carmichael (also known as Kwame Ture) and Charles Hamilton write: "This country also saw fit to treat German prisoners of war more humanely than it treated its own black soldiers. On one occasion, a group of black soldiers was transporting German prisoners by train through the South to a prisoner-of-war camp. The railroad diner required the black American soldiers eat in segregated facilities on the train—only four at a time and with considerable delay—while the German prisoners (white, of course) ate without delay and with other passengers in the main section of the diner!"

I present all of this at the onset so that one clearly understands my position as it relates to Western civilization. I view Western civilization through the lens of a victim of that civilization, not as a defender of Western civilization, so I certainly cannot share the alarm and concern that is expressed by Donald Trump and Patrick Buchanan. Moreover, I also will add that my position is that

Western civilization does indeed face a crisis, but that this is a self-inflicted crisis, although Trump and Buchanan obviously do not present it as such. Trump speaks of those who seek to destroy Western civilization, but historically the biggest threat to Western civilization has been itself. Buchanan himself exposes as much, which is actually the focus of my review.

Buchanan's view is that the large influx of immigrants coming into America is a threat to American civilization. To support this view he quotes Peter Heath, who wrote:

"In 376 a large band of Gothic refugees arrived at the Empire's Danube frontier, asking for asylum. In a complete break with established Roman policy, they were allowed in, unsubdued. They revolted, and within two years had defeated and killed the emperor Valens-the one who had received them-along with two-thirds of his army, at the battle of Hadrianople."

Based on this passage, Buchanan explains:

"What Valens had done was the Christian thing to do, but it had never been the Roman thing to do. Valens has his modern counterpart in George W. Bush. For in May 2006, Republican senators at Bush's urging joined Democrats to offer a blanket amnesty to 12 million illegal aliens. and permit U.S. businesses to go abroad and bring in foreign workers. Senators had been shocked by the millions of Hispanics marching in America's cities under Mexican flags. And as was the emperor Valens, President Bush was hailed for his compassion and vision."

Buchanan argues that the fall of Rome was the result of Rome becoming a multicultural society that incorporated foreigners who did not assimilate Roman values. This was perhaps one aspect of why Rome fell, but Buchanan also admits that the "barbarians" who conquered Rome were themselves conquered by Rome in the past:

"But these alien peoples brought with them no reverence for Roman gods, no respect for Roman tradition, no love of Roman culture. And so, as Rome had conquered the barbarians, the barbarians conquered Rome. In the fifth century, beginning with Alaric and the Visigoths in 410, the northern tribes, one after another, invaded and sacked the Eternal City. And the Dark Ages descended."

Buchanan is worried that America and Europe will suffer a similar fate to that of Rome in that the people who were formerly enslaved and colonized will invade Western civilization and gradually erode the values of that civilization. It is the concerns of people like Buchanan that was one of the reasons why Trump was elected. Trump understood the fears and insecurities that white society has over the threat that Western civilization faces, which was the message of the previously mentioned speech which Trump delivered in Poland.

An aspect of Western civilization's fragility is the ever present need to defend itself, whether militarily or morally. This is why Buchanan writes:

"Colonial rule was marked by such evils as chattel slavery and the exploitation of African labor in the mines of the Congo and South Africa. But was not the arrival of the West of immense benefit to the colonized peoples? Can Western civilization not Claim credit for having advanced all of mankind morally, politically, culturally between 1492 and 1960? Was not Western civilization vastly superior to the indigenous civilizations it encountered and crushed) from the Aztecs and Incas in the Americas to the Muslim, Hindu, Buddhist, Taoist civilizations from Africa to the Far East? Has not Western Man more to be proud of than ashamed of?"

This passage demonstrates the defensive nature of the West. Buchanan cannot merely state that slavery and colonialism were wrong, but he has to also offer a defense of Western civilization by speaking of the supposed good things that came out of colonization. The argument is essentially that slavery was bad, but that the West is still morally and culturally superior to the people that it murdered. What type of moral superiority is that? What type of culture is that?

Certainly, one finds warfare in Africa, but the destructive impulse that drives Western civilization was rarely to be found in Africa. One scholar writes of Africa's history: "Throughout their history, with the possible exception of the armies of Shaka Zulu, Africans had observed limits to the use of violence, sometimes even substituting ritual and symbol for physical force." But the morally superior Western world invaded Africa and committed several acts of genocide. This was done in the name of religion and civilization. It is noticeable that Buchanan attempts to downplay the worst aspects of colonialism, such as the millions that were massacred in Africa by European colonialists.

Buchanan also expresses issues with the United Nations conference which was held in South Africa in 2001: "In the first week of September 2001, in Durban, South Africa, a UN World Conference Against Racism, Racial Discrimination, Xenophobia and Related Intolerance was held. It quickly degenerated into an anti-white, anti-Western, anti-Israel jamboree. At the end a demand was made on the United States for reparations for the transatlantic slave trade."

Buchanan's view of world history is one in which the West has always been benevolent to the Third World. The various Western supported coups that toppled democratically elected governments around the world are not mentioned by Buchanan. Moreover, Buchanan complains that "Islamic nations that perpetuated slavery into the modern era, long after the Christian West had brought the evil to an end, were exempted from the reparations demands." Buchanan is oblivious to the fact that those who were raising the demands for reparations at the U.N. conference included activists such as Edna Roland, who descends from Africans who were enslaved by Europeans in Brazil. In other words, there was a specific reason for why Western countries were the target of the reparations claim during this conference.

The reason by Buchanan spends so much time in his book trying to defend the West or downplay the West's history of aggression against other people is because he fears that Western societies, particularly America, will become ashamed of its own history:

"Nor do Americans treasure the history or revere the heroes as we once did. What many still see as a glorious past, others see as shameful history. Columbus, Washington, Jefferson, Jackson, Lincoln, and Lee, heroes of the old America, are all under attack. To many, the discovery of America by the explorers from Columbus to Captain John Smith, and the winning of the West by pioneers, soldiers, and cowboys are no longer seen as heroic events but as matters of which Western man should be ashamed."

I do not think Western man needs to be ashamed, but let's be honest about the crimes committed by Western man against other people around the world. Buchanan writes: "Western society is afflicted with a guilty conscience. For Europeans, the guilt is over centuries of imperial rule. For Americans, it is guilt over our ancestors' injustices to the Native Americans and two centuries of enslavement of black Americans, followed by a century of segregation."

Buchanan is less concerned with the impact that Western imperialism has had on its victims and is instead concerned about this guilty conscience. He continues: "Our ancestors were not paralyzed by guilt. Confident in their culture and civilization, they believed in their superiority over what Kipling had called the 'lesser breeds without the law.' We come from a different people than the people we have become." Buchanan does not hesitant to acknowledge that President Andrew Jackson was a slave owner who viewed Native Americans as savages, that President Abraham Lincoln believed in white supremacy, or that Woodrow Wilson was a segregationist. Buchanan explains that "if racism means a belief in the superiority of the white race and its inherent right to rule other peoples, American history is full of such men."

Buchanan seems troubled that Westerners would look at their history of genocide, colonialism, and slavery with anything less than reverence. One issue that is apparent in his book is that Buchanan is incapable of viewing the world from the lens of those who were oppressed by Western civilization. He writes: "Growing up in the 1940s and 1950s, we did not feel any need to apologize for America's past, but took pride in all she had accomplished. African-Americans shared that pride." The 1950s was when the civil rights movement took off. African Americans at the time could not vote, go to an integrated school, or even drink from the same water fountain as white people, so one struggles to find this shared pride that Buchanan refers to.

One must give Buchanan some credit, however. He does not attempt to hide or cover up the racist nature of Western civilization. Instead, he argues that the technological and other advancements of the West offset the negatives. He complains that "though the achievements of our civilization in art, architecture, law, literature, technology, science, and governance, and the advance of human freedom and God-given rights eclipse those of any other, there has arisen among our intellectual and cultural elites a contempt for the West. Many see our ancestors as irredeemably racist, imperialist, and genocidal."

It is indeed true that over the last 500 years Western civilization has been one that has made many great advancements, but often at the cost of great human suffering. Buchanan attempts to maintain the curious position of trying to assert that Westerners should not feel ashamed of their history of imperialism, while also asserting the moral superiority and Christian values of the West. Which is it? Is Western civilization a morally superior civilization that places value on Christian ideals of peace and brotherhood, or is it a civilization that has no guilt for the destruction that it has caused? Buchanan boasts that Europeans were men "who went out from Europe to conquer and Christianize the world" because he wants to uphold both positions. In doing so, Buchanan provides support to an argument which was put forward by the psychologist Dr. Bobby E. Wright.

In his book, *The Psychopathic Racial Personality and Other Essays*, Dr. Bobby E. Wright presents Western civilization as a psychopathic civilization. Wright writes that because "of their lack of ethical or moral development there is no conflict between" Western religion and racism. Wright continues to explain that Europeans have "historically oppressed, exploited, and killed Black people, all in the name of their God Jesus Christ and with the sanction of their churches." Buchanan's attempts to defend Western civilization proves Wright's point that white people "have no mortality where race is the variable."

I also turn to another psychologist, Amos Wilson. In *The Falsification of Afrikan Consciousness: Eurocentric History, Psychiatry and the Politics of White Supremacy*, he criticized what he saw as the apparent normalization of European imperialism: "We know that imperialist Europeans stole nations and destroyed hundreds of thousands of Amerindians, Afrikans, and other peoples; and whose every step in other people's nations has done little but destroy the local people, drive them out of their minds, destroy their cultures, and rob them of their wealth. And yet, these people are held up as normal…"

In his book, Buchanan also mentions the controversy that emerged in France in 2005 when a law was enacted, which mandated that "school programs recognize in particular the positive character of the French overseas presence, notably in North Africa." The fact that Algeria fought a bloody war against France for their independence would suggest that Algerians certainly did not view French colonialism as something positive. Frantz Fanon came to support the struggle of the Algerian people when he saw how horribly they were being treated. President Abdelaziz Bouteflika of Algeria was not pleased by this new law. He said that the French "have no choice but to recognize that they tortured, killed, exterminated from 1830 to 1962," but Buchanan is not concerned with viewing the history of French colonialism in North Africa from the perspective of the Algerian victims. Buchanan explains: "But the ultimate issue here is not what foreigners or immigrants think of the history of France. The issue is what the French think, and whether the children of France shall be taught that their nation's history is glorious or sordid." Again, Buchanan only wants to view the world through the perspective of Europeans and not those who were oppressed by European colonialism.

Buchanan also expresses little interest in the cultures of non-Western people. Buchanan writes that in the 1960, African Americans "were not fully integrated into society, but they had been assimilated into our culture." He also writes: "We were of two races, but of one nationality: Americans." Buchanan fails to understand that this shared culture was not so much assimilation, but imposition. African Americans were enslaved and had Western culture imposed on them. Therefore, it seems to trouble Buchanan when he sees apparent rejections of Western culture on the part of African American who are seeking to reconnect with their African heritage. This is why he writes: "In the 1960s, black leaders from basketball great Lew Alcindor to boxing legend Cassius Clay, to poet Leroi Jones, to radicals like H. Rap Brown and Stokely Carmichael, began to adopt African and Islamic names to stress the degrees of separation from an American Christian mainstream."

Buchanan also references Shelby Steele, who explained: "No

group in recent history has more aggressively seized power in the name of its racial superiority than Western whites. This race illustrated for all time-through colonialism, slavery, white racism, Nazism-the extraordinary evil that follows when great power is joined to an atavistic sense of superiority and destiny. This is why today's whites the world over, cannot openly have a racial identity."

Steele continues to explain: "Black children today are hammered with the idea of racial identity and pride, yet racial pride in whites constitutes a grave evil. Say 'I'm white and I'm proud,' and you are a Nazi." I would argue that this is a bit of an exaggeration to suggest that white pride is necessarily seen as being evil. This is not a position that I maintain, but I will concede that Steele does have a point. The difference is, however, that the same legacy of racial superiority which Steele acknowledges is precisely why racial identity for white people is not the same as it is for black people. People such as Buchanan actually make it difficult for white people to assert a positive racial identity because he upholds the racists and takes the position that Westerners should not be ashamed to revere these racist imperialists. It is people like Buchanan who help to create the perception that racial pride among white people promotes racism.

Buchanan writes that "if black children are being 'hammered with the idea of racial identity and pride,' the 'color-blind society' of Dr. King's dream is dead." The problem is that Western society never accepted King's dream, which is why King endured being jailed on numerous occasions before he was finally assassinated. Given the manner in which Buchanan writes about Western history, I wonder if he even truly believes in King's dream.

I opened this piece by referencing Trump's remarks in Poland. As I have noted, both Trump and Buchanan share a common concern over the future of Western civilization. The central premise of *State of Emergency* is this need to protect the West from what Buchanan sees as an invasion.

It is ironic that Buchanan expresses so much concern about protecting America's borders and rule of law, when those were the very things which Europeans undermined when they went to

Africa. Contrary to how African history is sometimes presented, the rule of law did exist in Africa. Chancellor Williams gave the following description of how elders handled disputes in chiefless African societies. He writes: "Matters involving members of the same family or clan could be settled by the family council, each family or clan having its own elder. Conflicts between families or clans could be brought before any mutually acceptable elder for settlement. The elder's judgment was not binding on the parties to the dispute. [...] If the case was 'big' and serious and the disputants were dissatisfied with the elder's decision regarding it, they could call in one or more additional elders to hear and pass on the case." Williams points out that the elder's decisions were "advisory." This meant that the elders' judgment could be ignored, though Williams adds that "to ignore the elders was considered to be ignoring the community itself."

The king was also someone who maintained law and order. The absence of a king meant the absence of such law and order. Walter Rodney explained: "The intimate link between the king and the concept of law is demonstrated by the fact that the absence of a king, as in the interval between the death of one king and the crowning of the next, usually meant disorder and lawlessness." Rodney notes that during the period of civil strife over succession, the Papels of the Upper Guinea coast were known to have engaged in acts of robbery. Nicholas Owen, who was a slave dealer, recorded in 1757 that he heard news that the king of Sherbro was dead, but this news had not spread abroad because of the custom of keeping the death of a king hidden in order to make a new king "before any trouble ensues." Those last words were what Owen himself wrote. If there was no king present, then there was trouble.

In some cases, laws were represented by clan elders or by the king in societies with rulers. Maintaining law and order was sometimes a very delicate task because of the authority vested in certain figures and if that authority figure were to die, there would be no law and order until that position was replaced.

Western society has never been one to respect the borders or social orders of our civilizations. We see this in West Africa with Kwame Ansa, an African chief who responded to the Portuguese request to build a fortress on his land by saying that "it is far preferable that both our nations should continue on the same footing as they have hitherto done, allowing your ships to come and go as usual; the desire of seeing each other occasionally will preserve peace between us." Kwame Ansa recognized the potential for conflict if the Europeans attempted to settle in African lands and Ansa wanted to maintain the peace by keeping Europeans at a distance.

The Portuguese who came into West Africa demonstrated a disregard for many of the local laws and customs. Walter Rodney writes that "European traders took greatest exception to those African laws which had a direct bearing on European property." These laws stipulated that if a European trader died then his host would inherit the trader's property. This was a common law in the Upper Guinea Coast of West Africa. For example, if an animal fell dead in the domain of a specific ruler that ruler could then claim the animal, even if the animal was wounded outside of his territory by hunters who were not his subjects. Mansa Felupe, an African king, inherited the goods of all who died in his kingdom, as well as the property of his subjects that died in a foreign land. Walter Rodney explains that the Portuguese settlers "made strenuous attempts to change the nature of the agreements and to escape, in one way or another, from the authority of the African rulers."

The attempt to undermine the authority of the African rulers sometimes led to the instigation of conflicts between Africans. For example, some of the Portuguese who were living among the Banhun people were frustrated by the fact that they were being mistreated by the Banhun people. They invoked the support of King Masatamba, who attacked the Banhuns. The lack of regard for African customs and way of life was also demonstrated by Louis Binger, a French explorer. Binger said, and I quote: "I feel that a white man traveling in this country, whoever he may be, should not prostrate himself before a black king, however powerful the latter may be." He continued to explain that Europeans should "not have to bow their heads before indigenous chiefs to whom they are definitely superior in all respects." Europeans came into Africa as conquerors. They had no respect for the customs, laws, or territorial space of the people that they invaded.

Western civilization is one that has been very brutal in its conquests of others and seems to have a fear of falling victim to a similar type of invasion, but the reality is that much of the threats that Western civilization has faced has been self-inflicted. As Buchanan explained, it was other Europeans who destroyed Rome, but we can observe this pattern throughout Europe's history. The Greek city-states of Athens and Sparta fought a very brutal war against each other, known as the Peloponnesian War.

There were also the self-inflicted World Wars. Buchanan writes: "By 1918, the German, Austro-Hungarian, and Russian empires had collapsed. World War II bled and broke the British and French." These changes were caused not by invaders from the "Third World," but by Europeans fighting each other over global control over the world. The topic of World War returns us back to Trump's speech.

Trump framed his speech in Poland around this notion of defending Western civilization from threats. But what becomes apparent from listening to that speech is that much of the threat that Poland has faced was from other European people, other white people. Trump said: "In 1920, in the Miracle of Vistula, Poland stopped the Soviet army bent on European conquest. Then, 19 years later in 1939, you were invaded yet again, this time by Nazi Germany from the west and the Soviet Union from the east. That's trouble. That's tough."

Poland stopped an invasion from the Soviet Union and then nearly twenty years later was invaded by the Nazis. Trump is right. That is tough. These are white people fighting white people here. That is the trouble that Trump is referring to. Trump continues:

"Under a double occupation the Polish people endured evils beyond description: the Katyn forest massacre, the occupations, the Holocaust, the Warsaw Ghetto and the Warsaw Ghetto Uprising, the destruction of this beautiful capital city, and the deaths of nearly one in five Polish people. A vibrant Jewish population—the largest in Europe—was reduced to almost nothing after the Nazis systematically murdered millions of Poland's Jewish citizens, along with countless others, during that brutal occupation."

The imperialistic and destructive nature of Western civilization has not only been a danger to others, but it has been a danger to itself as well. Underneath this death and destruction is also a deep-seated feeling of inferiority and insecurity, which I have discussed at length. I will make reference to Marcus Garvey because Garvey clearly understood that the racism and oppression which African people experienced was rooted in this fear on the part of Europeans of losing their civilization to other people—precisely the same fear that Buchanan expressed in his book and that Trump expressed in his speech.

Garvey explained:

"Should you reverse the positions you would do the same thing as they did to us. Why do I say that? There is no man in this hall tonight—no Negro man or woman in this hall tonight—because all of us are human—who would for a whole life time labor and work himself industrially and thriftily to save everything that you possibly can to build up a home of your own and save a little fortune of your own to make yourself happy, and that after you did all that—you have your children; you have your own family to take care of and to look after with that which you individually worked for—there is no one of you who would go out into the street and see a tramp and take that tramp and bring him into your house and let him sleep in the same bed with you; let him occupy your drawing-room, let him enjoy all the comforts of it, and later on have him say to you, 'Let me tell you how to run your house.' There is no human being in this building who would do that. Yet that is what we expect the white man to do [...]."

What Garvey was explaining is that it is not realistic to expect white people to simply give their power to us. This desire to hold on to white domination in America is at the core of white supremacist thinking. Organizations such as the Ku Klux Klan and the Neo-Nazis reason that America is a country that was colonized and built by white people for white people, and they are not wrong in this view. The native people of the Americas were merely an obstacle to the building of this country. They had to be driven away so that the white colonizers could take their land. As for African people, we were the slave labor. That was the dynamic that founded this country. It was a country created by white people for white people.

The United States is a country that was founded on the principle of liberty, but there was never a doubt that this principle was intended for white people, especially wealthy white people. As such, African people have typically been on our own when it comes to engaging in certain struggles for equal rights. This was one of the issues that we saw in the American labor movement, which was really just a white labor movement. This was why in 1959 the black members of the American Federation of Labor and Congress of Industrial Organizations (AFL–CIO) had to form their own Negro American Labor Council (NALC) under the leadership of A. Philip Randolph. Randolph complained: "It is unfortunate that some of our liberal friends, along with some of the leaders of labor, even yet do not comprehend the nature, scope, depth, and challenge of this civil rights revolution which is surging forward in the House of Labor." The reality is that when you look at American history, you will find numerous examples of the white working class struggling for their own advancement with little regard to the struggles of African people.

When we look at what has taken place in America over the last ten years, we can understand why certain elements in the country are behaving as they are. First there was the economic collapse in 2008, in which many people lost their jobs and their houses. Economic insecurity is one of the pillars on which Donald Trump built his campaign. There are many white people in this country who are frustrated with their condition. They have lost their jobs and they feel as though they are losing their country. They witnessed the election of a black man named Barack Obama. Even worse than that, this was a black man with a Kenyan father and a white mother. White supremacist organizations like the Ku Klux Klan and the Nazis were always preoccupied with purity of blood, so it must have been an especially stinging blow to see a black man with a white mother take over the presidency of their country—as it is no doubt a blow to see Colin Kaepernick, another black man with a white mother, kneel to American anthem.

I do not sympathize with the Neo-Nazis and other white nationalist organizations that share their philosophies, but I understand their position and I understand their frustration. I reiterate that as far as these people are concerned America was founded by their white ancestors and they refuse to give up that country without a struggle. I quote Marcus Garvey again:

"Prejudice we shall always have between black and white, so

long as the latter believes that the former is intruding upon their rights. So long as white laborers believe that black laborers are taking and holding their jobs, so long as white artisans believe that black artisans are performing the work that they should do; so long as white men and women believe that black men and women are filling the positions that they covet; so long as white political leaders and statesmen believe that black politicians and statesmen are seeking the same positions in the nation's government; so long as white men believe that black men want to associate with and marry white women, then we will ever have prejudice, and only prejudice, but riots, lynchings, burnings, and God to tell what next will follow!"

This insecurity and this fear of losing power is one of the things that drove white racists to commit the atrocities against African people that they did, which is why Garvey's words here are so profound. Garvey understood that the European powers have no interest in sharing power or sharing wealth with African people. This same insecurity and fear are also one of the reasons why Trump was elected.

In conclusion, I will state that I agree with Buchanan's premise that Western civilization is in a state of emergency, but I would argue that this emergency is a self-inflicted one, not an emergency that was created by the "Third World" which Buchanan fears so much.

4 RACISM AND THE "MASTER RACE"

In *Mein Kampf*, Adolf Hitler wrote about how the eugenics laws in a number of American states were attempting to create a "master race." In a conversation, Hitler was quoted as stating: "I have studied with great interest the laws of several American states concerning prevention of reproduction by people whose progeny would, in all possibility, be of no value or be injurious to the racial stock."

Hitler not only studied American laws concerning eugenics, but American eugenicists also supported what was taking place in Nazi Germany at the time. Charles Goethe, who was an American eugenicist, took a number of trips to Germany. Following a trip to Germany in 1934, Goethe wrote a letter to another eugenicist named Ezra Gosney, explaining: "You will be interested to know… that your work has played a powerful part in shaping the opinions of the group of intellectuals who are behind Hitler… Everywhere I sensed that their opinions have been tremendously stimulated by American thought."

It should be little surprise that Nazis would look to America to find inspiration for their concept of developing a white "master race." From the very beginning, some of the founders of the United States believed in the notion of white supremacy. Thomas Jefferson, for example, wrote: "I advance it therefore as a suspicion only, that the blacks, whether originally a distinct race, or made distinct by time and circumstances, are inferior to the whites in the endowments both of body and mind".

This notion of a white "superior" race and other "inferior" races led to the genocidal violence against Native Americans. During the First Congress, both George Washington and Thomas Jefferson referred to Native Americans as savages.

European colonialists in North America often carried out the type of war against the Natives which Vattel had proscribed. Williams Trent, who was a trader at Fort Pitt during the Pontiac war, wrote that two Natives visited the fort. Trent wrote in his journal: "Out of our regard for them, we gave them two Blankets and an Handkerchief out of the Small Pox Hospital. I hope it will have the desired effect." The desired effect was clearly to spread smallpox among the Natives in an attempt to kill them off. Thomas Jefferson held the view that the "same world" would not do for both the Europeans and the Native Americans, and he suggested "extermination" as a remedy to this problem. Writings such as this clearly demonstrated that extermination of the Natives was the intent of some of the European colonialists.

The genocide of Jews which was carried out by the Nazis was justified under the doctrine that certain groups are superior and others are inferior. This is a doctrine which was not new by the time that Hitler came to power in Germany. In reality, the notion of superior and inferior races was the very thing which justified and sustained centuries of brutal violence against non-white people around the world. The example of violence against Native Americans was previously cited.

The doctrine of racial supremacy also played a role in the genocide which the Germans carried out in Namibia. The Herero people began rebelling against German injustices. They killed hundreds of German settlers within a matter of days. In response to these rebellions, German troops opened fire on an unarmed Herero mission station in Otjimbingwe, despite the fact that the Herero there were not even involved in the previous uprisings. Soon these revolts gave way to a war between the Germans and the Herero. The Herero did not want to pursue a long term war with the Germans, however. The Herero people moved away from the German settlements and hoped for a peace negotiation with the Germans. Instead of a negotiation, the Germans were preparing an army with the intention of wiping out the Herero people.

German propaganda was set up to gain public support for this massacre of the Herero people. The Germans made it appear as though the Herero were a savage and violent people that needed to be confronted with military force. German cartoons also depicted the Herero as being particularly violent towards white women, when this was not actually the case. At the Battle of Waterberg the Germans decisively defeated the Herero. The German general Lothar von Trotha then gave the infamous annihilation order. He planned the extermination of all the Herero people, claiming that he would no longer accept women or children.

Many of the Herero were driven into the desert where they died from starvation and thirst. It was also during this massacre that the Germans opened their first concentration camps. The Germans rounded up the surviving Herero and forced them into these camps. The Herero people were given a number and identified by this number. In these camps the Herero were used as slave labor. Many died of overwork and exhaustion. Others were shot or beaten. In these camps, food was scarce and the prisoners were given no medical care. The Nama people revolted against German rule and suffered the same fate as the Herero people had. This further demonstrates that the roots of Hitler's doctrine about the "master race" can be found in the history of racism against Africans and other peoples of the world. Of course, the people of Germany did not expect in the early 1900s that they would become victims of the type of atrocities which the German colonial empire was carrying out against the Herero people.